Designing Maintainable Software

Springer

New York
Berlin
Heidelberg
Barcelona
Hong Kong
London
Milan
Paris
Singapore
Tokyo

Dennis D. Smith

Designing
Maintainable
Software

With 14 Figures

 Springer

Dennis D. Smith
Information Science
3000 S.W. Avalon Way
Seattle, WA 98126
USA

Library of Congress Cataloging-in-Publication Data
Smith, Dennis D.
    Designing maintainable software/Dennis D. Smith
      p. cm.
    Includes bibliographical references.
    ISBN 0-387-98783-5 (alk. paper)
    1. Software maintenance. I. Title.
  QA76.76.S64S617   1999
  005.1'6—dc21   98-55412

Printed on acid-free paper.

Production managed by Frank McGuckin; manufacturing supervised by Jacqui Ashri.
Photocomposed copy prepared from the author's Microsoft Word files.
Printed and bound by Maple-Vail Book Manufacturing Group, York, PA.
Printed in the United States of America.

9 8 7 6 5 4 3 2 1

ISBN 0-387-98783-5 Springer-Verlag New York Berlin Heidelberg   SPIN 10713891

Preface

This book is about maintaining computer software. Its aim is to improve a program's capacity for altering code to fit changing requirements and for detecting and correcting errors.

The book is written primarily for systems analysts and programmers. But others will also find it interesting. Managers will find ways to decrease costs, improve the organization's performance, and lessen its liability exposure. Researchers will be given principles to expand upon, and will be able to develop techniques for solving new problems that arise in the world of maintenance. Another group to benefit is students. They will be given a foundation from which to write clear unambiguous programs.

Software maintenance is an important and timely area of investigation. It is the component that gives an information system its flexibility. It is also the source of many of its problems. Software is costly to maintain. It is the usual cause of system failures and is the frequently cited reason why systems operate in unintended ways. Most software problems are not serious and require only minor repairs. But some have resulted in the loss of significant physical and financial resources. Others have cost lives.

The book argues for a new way of thinking about maintaining software. Traditional approaches, using software engineering and management disciplines, do not adequately address maintenance issues. What is proposed to solve problems utilizes a set of human factors principles that govern the programmer-software-event world interactions and form the core of the maintenance process.

The real value and utility of the book lies in the principles that are proffered. Practical solutions, such as maintenance tools and cookbook procedures, are generally short-lived.

Principles can be applied to a variety of situations and lead to new insights into software maintenance.

The themes developed in the text are supported by applied and basic research. Each research enhances the credibility of the other, and both bring understanding to the problems of software maintenance. The practical applications of the principles are from programs the author has written and with which the author is most familiar.

Maintenance issues are presented, discussed, and addressed in a problem solving format. Stating maintenance goals and the criteria for meeting them creates a context for investigating the process and uncovering the principles that govern it.

Problems must be faced before they can be solved. Defining maintenance problems and deciding how to solve them are the topics of the first section. In Chapter 1 the problems created by software are described along with the maintenance process and its environment. Selecting an approach for solving the problems is the subject of Chapter 2. Chapter 3 discusses a model for interpreting the data amassed from the investigation, the software life cycle, and the method of attack used to bring about solutions.

The next two sections provide solutions for maintenance problems, and discuss the principles upon which they are based. Section II covers those solutions employing symbols. Chapter 4 begins the discussion by describing basic human information processing. In the three chapters that follow, the process of using and perceiving symbols is examined: Chapter 5, Naming; Chapter 6, Words and Letters; and Chapter 7, Abbreviations and Mnemonics. Language and how it is used is detailed in Chapter 8. Chapter 9, Language of Mnemonics, compares the differences between novice and expert programmers, and gives practical examples of how to apply the principles governing symbols.

Solutions involving the structure of programs are developed in the third section. Chapter 10 opens the section with a discussion on human problem solving. It is followed in Chapter 11 with the strategies and practices a programmer uses to maintain software. Software errors and the various barriers to maintenance are addressed in Chapter 12. Chapter 13 provides a number of structures that can be used to organize programs and code for effective maintenance.

Section IV is concerned with issues regarding solution implementation and testing. How the proposed solutions may be implemented in the development and maintenance phases of the software life cycle is explained in Chapter 14. Chapter 15 provides the reader with an overview of testing software. The section completes the problem-solving format.

Concluding Remarks, Chapter 16, makes up Section V.

The author gratefully acknowledges the contributions of Anthony Debons, Professor Emeritus at the University of Pittsburgh. His detailed examination of the first draft, advice, and encouragement have added greatly to the project. James Williams, Professor at the University of Pittsburgh, also made worthy suggestions. John Kraft provided legal advice.

Seattle, Washington   Dennis D. Smith

Contents

Section I
Facing the Problem

Chapter 1
The Problem

Throughout most of its life, software is being maintained. The period begins when the end user, or contracting agent, accepts responsibility for the program from its developers, and lasts until it is no longer considered useful. During this phase the program will have its capabilities enhanced and be corrected for errors many times. The purpose of this book is to extend the program's life by enabling these modifications to occur quickly and accurately, and to reduce maintenance expenditures.

Maintaining software is expensive. Most of the costs associated with programs occur after they have been developed (GSA, 1981; Glass & Noiseux, 1981; Vessey & Weber, 1983; Guimaraes, 1983; Gremillion, 1984; Bowen, Breuer, & Lano, 1993; Arthur, Nance, & Balci, 1993; Edelstein, 1993). Of the 100 billion dollars projected to be spent on software in the 1990s, only 30 billion will be for developing new programs. The remaining 70 billion will go towards program maintenance (Edelstein, 1993). Reducing maintenance costs is a primary reason why the maintenance process and the factors controlling its behavior need to be studied.

The importance of accurate and timely software maintenance is being recognized by the professional community. Prior to the late 1980s it had generated little interest (McClure, 1981; Chapin, 1986; Duncan, 1989; Abran & Nguyenkim, 1991; Robson et al., 1991; Bowen, Breuer, & Lano, 1993). Neither the programmer nor the manager highly regarded it (Babcock, 1987). Now the topic is addressed frequently, and there are conferences and a journal devoted to discussing maintenance issues. Many realize that software maintenance plays an important role in modern society (see Appendix A).

The Maintenance of Software

Keeping software working properly is a serious undertaking. Dangerous and costly situations caused by program failures have occurred frequently enough to raise concern over the use of software. Maintaining programs is difficult because software does not follow a well-known set of rules as does hardware (see Appendix B). Nevertheless software must be free of errors and operate safely in the environment for which it was created (Leveson, 1986, 1991).

Table 1. The Problem: Effects of Poor Software Maintenance.

- Routine maintenance is more expensive.
- May lead to failures that destroy equipment.
- Tends to hide design flaws that can injure people and cause deaths.
- Likely to contain errors that may result in huge financial loses.

The damage caused by ill-working software (see Appendix C) argues strongly for improvements in the maintenance process. To uncover the source of the problems, we must look beyond the symptoms and the perspective of the end user, and focus on the characteristics of programs, and the manner and environment in which software is maintained.

Program Characteristics

Some programs are easier to maintain than others: small programs are less trouble to modify than large programs; simple designs are better maintained than ones that are complex; and newly developed software has an edge over older or legacy programs. Within the software library, programs may also vary in language, application, and programming style. What makes programs difficult to maintain is a major concern of programming.

One area that needs to be examined is the maintenance of old programs. Over the years they have been modified many times and have grown in size and complexity. As a result they require more routine debugging when changes are made. Just locating the lines of code to be altered consumes 60% of the time spent on a modification request. And maintainers generally have little to help them in their task. Most often the authors of the code have left the department, and the documentation is either not available or is inaccurate. The code is often the programmer's only reliable source of information. Although it may be desirous to replace old software, it is usually not cost effective. Old programs contain valuable information and are worth billions of dollars (Lientz, 1980; Edelstein, 1993).

One characteristic that distinguishes a new program from an older one is its internal structure. Software that has been recently designed tends to be organized into hierarchical levels and has procedures that follow an input-process-output (HIPO) format. They may also be written in a language that lends itself to maintenance, such as one of the object-oriented languages or Ada. This generates a product that is delivered to the end user with fewer coding errors, and therefore allows more resources to be spent enhancing its capabilities and on other aspects of maintenance (Lientz, 1980).

However, the new entries into the program library are not without problems. Applications software is being written to function in environments that are more and more diverse. They are required to conform to a variety of operating systems and user interface protocols, and must create files that can be sent over a variety of networks. Because distributive processing is gaining popularity, application procedures may be spread over several computers not all of which are compatible. Procedures are now written in the "right" language. As a consequence, some jobs may have a number of different languages in use concurrently. There is also a proliferation of software development packages in which vendors have made outrageous productivity claims. In many cases these languages are proprietary. To further complicate matters, end user departments are writing their own software. These developments will only make the maintenance task more difficult (Grochow, 1993).

Another area that needs to be addressed is the deterioration of programs as they age. Software that has been altered many times through the years tends to lose the features that made it easy to maintain. Perhaps the most noticeable distinction between new and old software is the poor readability of the latter. When accepted, programs embody a singularity of thought. (Of course, that assumes the developers have been diligent in performing their duties.) They will have a consistent structure, a set of conventions for writing instructions, and one style of coding. As they age that order becomes less apparent.

Software grows as it is used. For new programs, a series of alterations is necessary to properly fit the programs into the end user's environment. As the end user initially explores the capabilities of the program, additional ways to use the software are discovered, requiring alterations to the code. Maintenance activity tapers off as the software becomes fixed in the end user's work routine. New programs expand at a faster rate and are modified more frequently than old software (Lientz, 1980).

The clarity of new software diminishes during maintenance. Programs are modified in stressful time-constrained situations that discourage detailed investigations into their construction. As changes are made, the risk of violating a naming convention, or adding to the complexity of an abstract mechanism is increased. Also, the responsibility for maintenance typically passes through a succession of programmers. And, each new maintainer tends to leave his imprint on the program segments on which he works. Updating support documentation, which is not one of the programmer's more relished chores, may not be accurate or done at all (Rombach, 1991). As a result, software inexorably becomes unprincipled, and continues to decline until it can no longer be understood (Martin & McClure, 1983; Edelstein, 1993).

The Maintenance Process

The administrative procedures used to manage software corrections and improvements are the maintenance process. Requests for maintenance vary in extent, complexity, scope, reason for change, and degree of urgency. An alteration may be straightforward and small, consuming only a few minutes of time. For major revisions, large portions of the code will be affected. These can be very complicated, produce errant code, and require a number of programmers working full time over several months to implement (Collofello & Gosalia, 1993).

Program maintenance becomes necessary to correct errors in the code, to implement changes in the end user's data and processing requirements, and to enhance software performance. In the software engineering literature these respective categories are known as corrective, adaptive, and perfective modifications (Glass & Noiseux, 1981; Abran & Nguyenkim, 1991; Pickard & Carter, 1993). A better interpretation of maintenance requests is to view them as reactions to changes in the environments, or event worlds, of the end user and the programmer.

Actually all maintenance requests are adaptive. Some will originate within the end user's event world, such as an additional report to inform management of the sales of a new product line, or updates to employment files. They are in response to changes that have occurred in the applications domain. Therefore, what is really being done when " adaptive" requests to software are performed is applications maintenance.

Maintenance requests may also reflect changes occurring within the software department. Events such as the purchase of a new compiler or an operating system may require coding alterations. Modifications will certainly be necessary to implement a more efficient algorithm or to restructure the code to improve its maintainability. "Perfective" modifications both improve the quality of the code and retain its integrity in changing computer/software configurations or platforms. In this capacity the programmer is engaged in coding maintenance.

Errors may be introduced into a program through either applications or coding maintenance. It is advantageous to view errors as two maintenance types rather than grouping them as "corrective" changes. Error causes differ with respect to the environment in which they originated. Applications maintenance errors can usually be traced to a faulty specification. End users are not always able to clearly express their intentions in terms of system capabilities. Ill-defined requests and misunderstandings between the end user and the information specialist or systems analyst are principal causes of these types or errors. Coding errors are caused by improperly translating the requirements of the end user into computer instructions. Each error type needs to be treated differently.

The end user approves the schedule for implementing maintenance requests. The degree of urgency, scope, size, number of man hours, and availability of resources all factor into the decision. Most requests can be planned. Minor changes are performed when it is convenient. Likewise, errors that do not have a significant impact on the end user may have their effects minimized through a workaround, be corrected along with other modifications, or be left as is. Major revisions are the most difficult to schedule. The time allotted to implement them cannot be accurately estimated, and is usually inadequate to complete the job. Errors that endanger life, destroy property, or cause financial loss are resolved immediately. The programmer will be at work on the problem until the error is found and corrected.

Maintenance programming can be very stressful. Programmers frequently work under pressure, whether it is to meet a deadline for a major revision or to respond to an emergency requiring an exigent alteration to the code (Gorla, 1991).

The Maintenance Environment

The environment in which programs are maintained affects the quality and timeliness of software modifications. Poor working conditions do not attract skilled programmers, add stress, and can lead to injuries such as carpal tunnel syndrome.

For example, in large software departments, programmers can be assigned to desks within a large office bay. There the ambience tends to be noisy and filled with many distractions. Concentrating on a maintenance task at times will be difficult. Within bays, work space is limited. Rarely is there sufficient room to spread out compiler listings and support documentation. Needed equipment may not be available. Maintainers usually must vie with others for resources in pools. Also, the equipment used may not be ergonomically designed causing discomfort and often leading to injury. A poor working environment can only increase the cost of maintaining programs.

Maintenance Tools

The effectiveness of software tools to expedite the maintenance process depends on the size and complexity of the program, the modification to be performed, and the skill of the maintainer. The preferred tools are the compiler listing and the text editor. Tools designed to assist the programmer in debugging software are not widely used (Gould, 1975), at least for small programs.

However, many programs now contain over a million lines of code and have complex abstract mechanisms. For these, sophisticated tools are required to navigate through the code and display its operations.

The maintenance process has benefited from the productivity tools created for software developers. Analysis and design tools improve the quality of software. As a result, maintenance tasks have been shifting from correcting errors to enhancing capabilities (Lientz, 1980, 1983).

The Maintainer

The programmer is the key to well-maintained software. His job is to keep programs operating to the end user's satisfaction. After a program has been written and accepted, the maintainer has the responsibility of correcting the errors and altering the code. Without the maintainer to make these adjustments, computer software would fall into a state of disrepair and disuse. In spite of this worthy contribution, the maintainer has the lowest esteem within the programming profession.

Maintenance programmers have mixed backgrounds. Their experience and training vary considerably. Maintainers may have spent several years in the field practicing their craft, or be at their initial programming assignment. Some will be highly educated, possessing undergraduate and graduate degrees. Others will have at most a technical or high school diploma. Most need training in their duties. But training is not generally provided by management (Chapin, 1986).

Having a computer science degree or being certified does not guarantee that a programmer knows how to maintain software. Computer science curricula have largely neglected training in this area (Bowen, Breuer, & Lano, 1993), and those proposed do not include maintenance courses (Magel et al., 1981; Eerkes,

1991). Although there have been attempts to give programmers professional status through certification (Neumann, 1991), testing does not cover software maintenance. There are no standards for maintenance that are universally accepted by the professional community.

Careers in programming typically begin by maintaining computer software. Maintenance is considered a relatively harmless activity where entry-level programmers can become proficient in the craft (Gorla, 1991; Rombach, 1991). While in maintenance, programmers are expected to obtain a thorough understanding of the department's software conventions, the idiosyncrasies of computer equipment, and the company's culture and methods of operation. Programmers in maintenance are aware that they are at the bottom of the professional hierarchy and look forward to leaving their present assignment. Maintainers demonstrating superior ability advance into the more creative positions, such as development programmer, systems analyst, or information specialist. Others migrate to different positions within the company, or gain employment in another concern where the rewards and opportunity for professional growth are more promising. The rest have maintenance as a career. That leaves the task of keeping software properly functioning to programmers who are poorly motivated, have low esteem, and possess marginal skills (Glass & Noiseux, 1981).

Programmers work differently in maintenance than when developing software. In the latter, they are part of a team headed by a lead programmer. The team functions as a unit and, through a massive concentrated effort, creates a software product. In contrast, maintenance programmers frequently work alone (Glass & Noiseux, 1981). Only three or four programmers may be needed to maintain large programs. Another difference is that the jobs maintainers receive generally do not involve extensive revisions to the code. Modifications tend to be small and limited in scope, and are proposed as needed. Also, the requests for alterations arrive sporadically. There are periods where a programmer is very busy and intervals in which no changes are scheduled.

Therefore, many programmers have other duties to perform. As in development, software maintainers are expected to meet the requirements of the end user. This, like most other duties in maintenance, is performed more easily and more accurately if the programmer was involved in the software's development (Lientz, 1980).

Maintainers normally perform a variety of tasks. Procedures in maintenance differ from those of development only in scale. Maintenance programmers may be asked to do any of these tasks even though most have had no experience developing software. Updating support documentation and end user training may also be included in their responsibilities.

Personality and character traits factor into the programmer's ability to maintain software. Chief among these are flexibility, versatility, and diplomacy. For example, flexibility is required to retain the developer's programming style for each program in the software library. The maintainer must adjust to differing styles, resisting any temptation to add another imprint to the initial expression of the design. Programs containing multiple styles are more troublesome to repair. Maintainers also need to be versatile. There are many different tasks to perform and programmers must contend with several computer languages. Within the program library there may be software written in FORTRAN, LISP, or C++. Maintainers should be proficient, or be able to learn quickly, each language used in the software department. Diplomacy is required to interact with end users. When end users have a software problem or request, they may, depending on the organization of the software department, bring it to the maintenance programmer. Good relations with the end user will eliminate many of the social problems that can arise (Glass & Noiseux, 1981).

The Software Department

The size of the software department and the philosophical direction of management determine how maintenance tasks will be assigned. In a small department, consisting, for example, of two programmers and two data entry clerks, all personnel are expected to perform a variety of duties. This is particularly true for programmers. Typically, one of them will assume the managerial duties of the shop. However, he also will be required to develop specifications, design software, write programs, and maintain a portion of the software library. The other programmer will have a number of responsibilities as well. He may be expected to run software packages for clients, develop and write a few programs, and take on the larger share of the maintenance tasks.

The many resources of a large software department allow the programmer to specialize in one or more areas, and the manager to concentrate on overseeing the affairs of the organization. Software personnel may be deployed in several ways. The primary distinction is whether software development and maintenance activities are combined or are performed within separate units. Neither structure has a clear advantage over the other, although a separate maintenance section will maintain software in fewer programmer man-hours (Glass & Noiseux, 1981).

Table 2. The Causes: Factors Contributing to Poorly Maintained Software.

- Software complexity, age, and size.
- Programming style.
- Use of different programming languages.
- Time constraints.
- Stress.
- Nonexistent or poor support documentation.
- Imprints from many programmers.
- Poor working environment.
- Lack of maintenance training.
- Maintenance programmers lack status, have low self-esteem, and may be ill-suited to the task.
- High turnover in personnel.

Concomitant with size is bureaucracy. Large software departments are wont to formalize the procedures used to control the maintenance process. The methods will vary among organizations according to the preference of management. They have no effect however on the accuracy or efficiency in which changes are implemented (Glass & Noiseux, 1981).

Summary

We now live in the information age. Modern society has become reliant on the systems that generate and transport data used to create information. At the heart of these systems is computer software. Properly maintaining software is crucial to ensuring that these systems can be reliably used. When software fails, huge financial losses, and even death may result.

Maintaining software is not highly regarded. Programmers working in that capacity have little esteem, and are considered to be at the low end of the programming hierarchy.

Software is maintained to allow it to adapt to the changing environments of the end user and the software department. Some adaptations however are unwanted. More commonly referred to as errors, they are caused by faulty specifications and requirements, or incorrect translations of the design into code.

Large programs are difficult to maintain. As they are modified they increase in size and complexity. Software that had been designed with a singularity of thought will, through the course of time, become imprinted with the various styles of its maintainers. This is due in part to the pressures created by deadlines and emergency situations, which do not encourage the programmer to study the code in detail. The deterioration of a program's structure and conventions for writing instructions is inevitable.

Chapter 2
The Approach

Descriptions of the software maintenance environment and definitions of the problems encountered provide a base from which to look for solutions. The search will be more efficient if an approach is adopted. The approach establishes a framework for solving problems, and hastens a conclusion whereby the causes of the problems are eliminated or are made less severe.

Problem solving is discussed many times throughout this book. It is the means by which maintainable designs for software will be produced. It is also the primary activity in which the programmer is engaged. For an introduction to the topic, please refer to Appendix D.

Approach Definition

The approach provides the general means for resolving problems. A search for a solution may proceed in several plausible directions. Usually it is not feasible to pursue each possibility. An approach significantly reduces the number of solution paths to consider, and allows more resources to be focused on those paths showing the most promise. Approaches arise naturally as solution proposals are grouped according to the tactics they employ.

Chapter Overview

In this chapter three approaches are considered: the managerial approach which resolves problems by manipulating human and material resources, the engineering approach in which solutions emanate from the surface regularities found in program code, and the cognitive approach which develops solutions from an understanding of a programmer's cognitive representations and processes. Each approach is assessed according to its potential for addressing the fundamental problems inherent in maintenance programming.

The Managerial Approach

The dictionary[1] defines management as:

> The conducting or supervising of something (as a business). -Esp: The executive function of directing, controlling, and supervising any industrial or business project or activity with responsibility for results.

To put it another way, management is the entity that exerts control over the human, material, and financial resources of an organization or operation, and bears the responsibility for achieving its goals and objectives. Within the software department, managers have duties that are both common to most supervisors, such as hiring, firing, motivation, and the like, and unique to the programming field, such as time estimates for software projects, assessing advancements in technology, training, and so forth. The issues they consider to be important are planning and organization of software projects (GSA, 1981, 1983a, 1983b), reducing expenditures (Guimaraes, 1983), user education (Lientz, 1980), increasing programmer productivity (Lientz, 1980), producing quality software (Fried, 1982), effective utilization of programming resources (Lientz & Swanson, 1981; Lientz, 1983), assessing the capacity requirements of computing machinery, and providing reliable hardware and software.

Management, because it controls the resources and prioritizes work, is responsible for bringing about the constructive changes needed in the way software is maintained. Managers typically think, operate, and assign tasks in general terms. When a more detailed analysis is required, specialists are called in (Glass & Noiseux, 1981; Lewis, 1989). Working in this manner, there are four ways the manager can affect software maintenance. One is through motivation and improving the programmer's working environment. Motivation is needed to combat the maintainer's low self-esteem (Babcock, 1987) and the tedious nature of the job. Another is by the acquisition of more effective development methodologies and software tools. For example, the use of structured software techniques will enable the programmer to make alterations more quickly and accurately. Setting up training courses on maintenance is a third way (Chapin, 1986). Training in most places amounts to an introduction to the computing facilities, the software library, and the support documentation. What is needed is a course on how to maintain computer software, and how to write programs that are easy to modify. The fourth is by developing a more effective research program (Lientz, 1983; Bowen, Breuer, & Lano, 1993). Managers need to increase funding, and establish a dialogue with scientists to identify topics for investigation.

---

[1] *Webster's Third New International Dictionary*, Philip Babcock Cove, Editor, Merriam-Webster, Inc., Springfield, Mass., 1986.

The Engineering Approach

Using this approach, solutions to the maintenance problems are attained by measuring and manipulating the surface features of computer software. Two disciplines that employ these means are software engineering and software science. The approach has a large number of adherents. Many believe that it has significantly contributed to the art of programming. Software engineering is an interdisciplinary field of study that utilizes mathematics, engineering techniques, and management science to solve program development problems. Its objectives are to reduce the cost and complexity of software, and make it more reliable and easier to maintain. Software engineers are interested in algorithm analysis, cost estimation, risk assessment, personnel coordination, and the management of software projects.[2]

It is perhaps through requirements engineering that the discipline will make its most important contribution to maintenance programming. Requirements engineering is the development of clear, precise, and unambiguous specifications. This is the first step that is taken in creating a program, and affects all of the other phases of development (i.e., design blueprint, code implementation, and test and validation). A substantial portion of the problems that surface in maintenance can be traced to faulty requirements engineering (Brooks, 1987). To lessen the impact of specification anomalies, software engineers have developed formal requirements specification languages (Leveson, 1991) designed to detect lapses in consistency, establish a means for controlling a program's configuration, and provide a way for tracing certain relationships throughout a program. When the specifications are error free, a sound foundation is provided from which a program can be constructed and maintained.

Software engineers have made other contributions to maintenance programming. They include assessing software maintainability (Vessey & Weber, 1983; Berns, 1984; Gremillion, 1984), developing predictors of software readability (DeYoung, Kampen, & Topolski, 1981; Elshoff & Marcotty, 1982), identifying factors contributing to repair maintenance (Lientz, 1980, 1983; Lientz & Swanson, 1981), and creating maintenance tools and aids (Kaiser, 1988).

The discipline, however, has attracted a number of critics. It has been in general characterized as a discipline that arrives at conclusions casually, through self-inspection (Brooks et al., 1983). When it has presented controlled experiments for consideration, there has been much concern over the methodologies employed (Moher & Schneider, 1982). What bothers the detractors are the types of subjects, computer languages, and program lengths used in the experiments.

Using subjects, differing in programming abilities, is problematic because they do not write or interpret software in the same way. Therefore, the results of experiments that use inexperienced programmers as subjects may not apply to experts. Programming skill is thought to determine the types of software errors committed, the rate at which errors are discovered, and the procedures chosen to perform programming tasks (Moher & Schneider, 1982). Also, investigators

---

[2] *Encyclopedia of Computer Science and Engineering*, Second Edition, Anthony Ralston, Editor, Van Nostrand Reinhold, New York, 1983.

frequently used college and graduate students as subjects. But these subjects do not reflect the commercial populations that maintain software. Therefore one has to question the value of those experiments (Moher & Schneider, 1982; Banker et al., 1993).

The second criticism is essentially a philosophical dispute. Languages employed in research vary in complexity and sophistication. Experimenters may study natural languages (e.g., English), programming languages (e.g., FORTRAN), or highly constrained languages designed for a specific purpose. Some contend that highly constrained microlanguages allow the investigator to focus on a specific area of interest apart from other language problems. There are other scientists who believe constrained languages are too restrictive for gaining practical insights. They think research should concentrate on improving languages programmers actually use (Gannon, 1976; Moher & Schneider, 1982).

The size of the program determines the credibility of the conclusions drawn from some experiments. Some classes of problems, such as syntax, may be unaffected by program size. Others will become evident only in programs beyond a certain length. The results of experiments using small programs (i.e., under 100 lines of code) need to be interpreted carefully (Gannon, 1976; Schneiderman, 1976; Moher & Schneider, 1982; Banker et al., 1993).

Software Science

Software science was developed by Maurice Halstead to measure software performance. He wanted to transform computer programming from an art to a science, and created a system of metrics based on mathematics and psychological experiments to achieve that purpose. The definitions found in Appendix E illustrate the means he employed, and the issues he intended to address.

Software science, as with software engineering, is flawed. The tenets proposed by Halstead are based on assumptions and misinterpretations of controlled experiments in psychology. Questioned specifically by his critics are his applications of short-term memory (see Appendix E) capacity to parameter lists, the validity of the Stroud Number (STM), and the method of search employed by people for retrieving information (Black & Sebrechts, 1981; Curtis, 1981; Coulter, 1983; Curtis et al., 1984).

To discuss the criticisms of software science, a rudimentary understanding of sensory input processing is necessary. Curtis et al. (1984) in Appendix F provide the basics.

The first two criticisms of software science (i.e., limiting the number of parameters for a module to the capacity restrictions of STM and the use of the Stroud Number in determining the amount of time required to write a program) claim that Halstead misinterpreted the sensory processing experiments of Miller (1956) and Stroud (1955). Halstead suggested that a routine's parameters and calling arguments be limited to five inputs and one output. His critics contend that parameters and calling arguments are recalled from LTM (long-term memory), not STM, and are therefore not restricted in number. Lengthy parameter lists (e.g., Smith, 1981) may not hinder program understanding. The validity of the Stroud Number is also questioned. Stroud reported the processing rate of items as a range of values. The success Halstead had with a number (18) lying within that range is coincidental (Coulter, 1983). Also, the unit that undergoes cognitive processing is the chunk. Tabulations of operators and operands are extremely fine-grained measures (Curtis et al., 1984). Finally, both Miller and Stroud employed simple experimental designs. Their results may not extend to the more involved tasks performed by the programmer (Black & Sebrechts, 1981; Coulter, 1983; Curtis et al., 1984).

The last criticism of software science attacks the assumption that human memory searches are binary. This is simply not the case (Coulter, 1983; Curtis et al., 1984). In STM an exhaustive serial search is used (Coulter, 1983). Nor are binary searches employed in LTM. There, information is accessed by cueing chunks.

In summary, Halstead's measures would be more useful if they were designed to reflect the semantic complexities of program code (Black & Sebrechts, 1981; Mynatt, 1984). In their present state, they can be compared to the reading formulae of the 1950s that were also based on textual regularities (Black & Sebrechts, 1981). Those measures failed to consider the reader's cognitive processes and were consequently outperformed by metrics sensitive to content. This pattern appears to be repeating. Metrics for programs based on chunks have already been proposed (Davis, 1984).

The Cognitive Approach

The cognitive approach encompasses those disciplines that seek to understand the human condition and apply the knowledge acquired towards making the interaction of people and things more efficient and safe. In software it means designing interfaces and code to improve the performance of the end user and maintainer.

The cognitive approach is essentially software ergonomics or human factors. The name was chosen to reflect a new attitude towards program design. The use of ergonomics traditionally has been to enhance a program's capacity for human interaction after it has been written. For example, a completed program is run through a "pretty print" routine to make it more readable. What is meant by the cognitive approach is that now human characteristics are considered in the design process and not as an afterthought. It signifies a fundamental shift in thinking about software.

Information Science

Information science is one discipline of the cognitive approach. It can be roughly defined as the examination and representation of thoughts as they are conceived, communicated, and comprehended by another person. The bounds of the field and the salient elements within it are laid out in the knowledge spectrum of Anthony Debons et al., (1988).

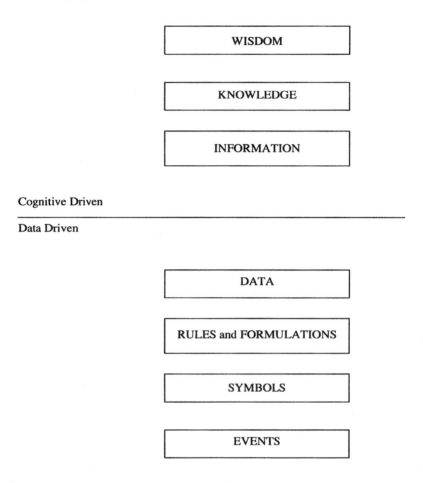

Figure 1. The Knowledge Spectrum of Debons et al.

Debons et al. make a point to separate components that are data driven from ones that are cognitive driven. The former includes, in ascending order, events, symbols, rules and formulations, and data. Comprising the latter are information, knowledge, and wisdom. Events are the changing states that occur within the world. They are represented by symbols (i.e., pictures, words, numbers, etc.). Rules and formulations organize symbols, and in so doing generate data. Sentences and mathematical formulae are two examples of how data can be created. The cognitive driven segment begins when a person senses data or becomes informed. Information is defined as the cognitive state of being aware of some event. It is that and nothing more. At the next higher level (knowledge) is the ability to understand situations, analyze problems, and apply information to resolve issues in the event world. The spectrum is bounded by wisdom. Wisdom is the judicial use of knowledge. Reason, values, and ethics are ways knowledge can be regulated. The wise use of knowledge elevates the practitioner and others affected by the act. Beyond wisdom lies possibly the domain of the spirit. Matters pertaining to the spirit are understood through faith. They are beyond the realm of science and, by definition, lie outside the knowledge spectrum.

Practitioners of the discipline solve problems by administering to the information and knowledge needs of the individual. That may require providing a client with additional information, eliminating noise or unwanted information, extending a person's information processing capabilities, reformatting data, or altering the information flow. Information scientists study how people use symbols and how they process the knowledge spectrum components to increase their understanding of the world. Solutions are developed by revising the way symbolic material is processed, stored, retrieved, transported, or interpreted (Debons et al., 1981; Flynn, 1987).

Information science is an interdisciplinary field of study. This character is evident in its foundation, the manner in which basic research is conducted, and the approach practitioners take to solve problems. At its core are four areas of learning:

> philosophy—logic, epistemology, and methods of inquiry;
> mathematics—statistics and probability;
> linguistics—event classification and communications; and
> behavioral sciences—psychology in all forms and sociology.

Its fundamental principles are developed by synthesizing contributions primarily from the core areas of study and through controlled experiments. They are stated in general terms. Practitioners have studied the basic principles of the field, and are able to apply them to specific situations. One of their roles is to assemble and relate items of information. Practitioners will make use of a number of resources to satisfy an information demand. After an analysis has revealed which topics need further study and the topics have been researched, the accumulated findings are synthesized and worked into a coherent solution that is practical and robust. One advantage of using an interdisciplinary approach is that an input from one source can be used to confirm a tenet from another (Debons, Horne, & Cronenwith, 1988).

Discussion and Summary

Deciding on an approach is an important step towards solving a problem. It enables solutions to be obtained more efficiently, and becomes a necessity when the problem can be solved by different means and there seem to be a number of potential solutions. An approach narrows the solution paths for consideration to those showing the most promise, and thereby allows more resources and energies to be focused on other problem-solving activities. Three approaches to the maintenance problems have been described. Before discussing the merits and drawbacks of each, the basic nature of the problem to be solved should be understood and expressed, and the criteria for a solution be made known. The more precisely a problem is defined, the more obvious the decision will be.

The Nature of the Problem

The maintenance problems to be solved are, in essence, impairments to a programmer's ability to effectively maintain software. They are most apparent in large programs, and can be dichotomized roughly into primary and ancillary issues. Comprising the former category are problems faced by the programmer as he develops, interprets, and modifies a set of computer instructions. They are concerned with how the programmer(s) uses, perceives, and generates software. A programmer will encounter a number of obstacles when maintaining software. Chief among them are the enormous size of some programs, multiple programming styles, and conflicting coding conventions. Ancillary issues are other problems hindering a programmer, such as those in the working environment (e.g., excessive office noise, lack of motivation, too much stress, etc.), software tools, and the organization of the software department.

Solution Criteria

Solutions will be acceptable if they remove or reduce the severity of programming impediments without creating new problems. Included in the criteria are end user considerations. That is, software must be modified and corrected, quickly and accurately. Solutions to the maintenance problems will principally enhance the programmer's ability to locate sections of code, comprehend their functions, and make alterations.

Managerial Approach

In the managerial approach, solutions are generated through stating and meeting goals, allocating resources, and identifying problems. Managers have the greatest influence on the maintenance process. Therefore, the primary responsibility for addressing problems within the process lies with them. These responsibilities include eliminating situations that are hazardous, financially draining (due to a catastrophic failure), or inefficient, organizing resources to effect solutions, and taking the initiative to prevent problems from occurring (e.g., training maintenance personnel).

A characteristic of managers is that they tend to conduct their business in generalities. Rarely do they concern themselves with the underlying causes of problems. Managers may improve the maintainer's working environment, purchase software tools, and reorganize the software department. But, these are not central to the maintenance problem. Even then the manager may need to consult with experts to bring forth solutions. Those in command of organizations usually do not possess a technical background. Their lack of familiarity with the details of software development and maintenance (Glass & Noiseux, 1981) is the reason the approach is not considered. Managers who do not understand the art of programming will have difficulty recognizing a problem, and therefore cannot be expected to have the competence to define and solve one. Their attempts at problem solving frequently consist of nothing more than throwing resources in its general direction. A caricature of the approach, the monkey approach to maintenance programming,[3] captures the folly of using it. In the monkey approach, the manager hires an infinite number of programmers, primates, and people off the street to write programs, sets them in front of an infinite number of computer terminals, and expects them, given an infinite amount of time, eventually to arrive at the sought-after modification. All the manager has to do is monitor the progress of those using the terminals.

An area where managers could improve maintenance is in training (Chapin, 1986). However, what they consider training typically consists of learning a new programming language or software tool. Courses that teach the principles of maintenance programming are few.

An additional drawback of the approach is that some managers may apply economic theory to maintenance problems. Economic theory does not adequately address the information needs of the programmer. Predictions of an actor's behavior are based on his interaction with his environment and are independent of his cognitive processes. It is assumed that actors make decisions that will give them the maximum utility in the present situation (Simon, 1990).

Engineering Approach

The engineering approach uses the surface features of programs to develop solutions for maintenance problems. Two disciplines falling within this approach are software engineering and software science. They employ techniques that were either borrowed from the engineering fields, or were developed from misinterpretations of experiments in psychology. Both disciplines are inadequate for resolving maintenance problems. Software science proffers a collection of erroneous tenets and faulty assumptions. Correlations between their predictions and actual results are coincidental. The latter discipline is discarded because the algorithms and mathematics used in engineering applications are inappropriate for solving human perception and cognitive problems. Furthermore, adherents of software engineering seem to be more interested in making machines and supervisors efficient than in enhancing the productivity of maintenance programmers. Software engineering is most useful to maintenance in testing software, and for detecting duplicate and inconsistent code.

Cognitive Approach

The cognitive approach employs knowledge from the behavioral sciences and other disciplines to solve maintenance problems. Information science is one area

---

[3] Inspired by a Bob Newhart comedy routine.

of learning encompassed by this definition, and is the approach through which the solutions will be pursued. The discipline is capable of producing satisfactory solutions. It is the best choice among the alternatives because it directly confronts the problems faced by the maintainers and promises solutions that will be practical and robust.

Chapter 3
The Attack

The attack refers to the strategy and tactics used to resolve problems. It is a plan of action employed to direct the investigation of issues raised in the problem domain. Plans are developed within the bounds of the approach and use its vocabulary. Therefore, the plan proposed will seek to meet the information demands of the software maintainer.

The first section of the chapter describes an information processing model. As the plan is carried out, information will be produced and become incorporated into the model. Its purpose is to provide a framework for discussing the problem. Through it events will be defined, root causes pursued, and solutions developed.

Next, the model is applied to software maintenance situations. Since maintenance problems may originate in any phase of the software's life cycle, the cycle is first defined. Then each phase is examined with respect to the interactions among the information systems within it. How programs, and the people who create and maintain them, process information must be understood throughout the program's cycle.

The plan of attack is discussed in the third section. It consists of the method of inquiry for bringing applicable information and knowledge to bear on the problems, and includes the procedures used to generate solutions.

EATPUT—An Information Processing Model

Maintenance programmers do not always receive the information required to perform their tasks. Information may be needed that is not contained in the program or support documentation, there may be trouble accessing it because it is intermingled with other data, or it may not be recognized in its present form. Meeting the programmer's information needs is the primary goal of the investigation.

Programmers and end users consume and generate information. That is, they function as information systems. Knowing how information systems operate is essential for modeling the behavior of information consumers, and for utilizing the knowledge gathered from the plan of attack. A useful model for achieving this is the EATPUT system.

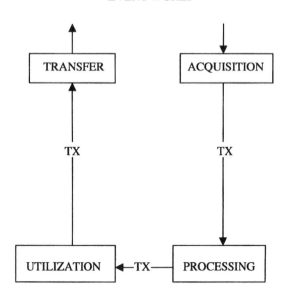

Figure 2. Debons's EATPUT Model.

EATPUT is a general model of the information system developed by Anthony Debons, Ester Horne, and Scott Cronenweth (1988). It may be used in a wide range of situations to describe information processing.

1. *Event world*: the objects and actions found in the external environment of the information consumer.
2. *Acquisition*: the apparatus used for sensing or capturing representations of objects and actions in the event world.
3. *Transmission (TX)*: the passage of data or signals from one component of the system to another.
4. *Processing:* storing, structuring, and retrieving data.
5. *Utilization*: the evaluation of information and/or knowledge, and its application towards the achievement of some goal.
6. *Transfer*: information is sent into the event world to be used by other information consumers.

The model operates recursively, and may represent an information system at different levels of granularity. Used in a general sense, it will depict the overall processing system. But it may also be employed to describe each component within the system (see Appendix G).

For maintenance issues, the EATPUT system will be used to model various processing systems that factor into the creation and upkeep of software. Chief among these are those of the end user and software maintainer. Although both have an interest in the same applications programs, their relationship to software differs.

In the end user's system, information and knowledge are utilized to achieve the goals set forth within the applications domain. The purpose of software is to assist him in reaching those goals. An end user is mainly concerned with how to interact with the computer system in order to get it to produce a desired output. Applications programs may augment each component of the end user's EATPUT system.

Note that a computer system may also be interpreted as an information processing system. It has an event world (the end user) and an acquisition component (keyboard, touch screen, etc.), and it electronically transmits signals between components, processes data (e.g., sorts data and stores the rearranged items on disc), utilizes data (performs calculations, make decisions, etc.), and transfers symbols to the end user.

The maintainer's information processing system is directed at modifying applications software (i.e., the processing and utilization components of the computer system). Its purpose is to alter software in ways that enhance the EATPUT system of the end user. The principal elements in this event world are the coded instructions of the applications program and the request to modify it. Information transfer is achieved primarily through the revised operation of the end user's software.

APPLICATIONS   MAINTENANCE

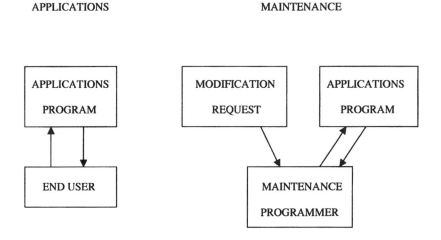

Figure 3. Information Systems in Maintenance.

Software Life Cycle

Obstructions to maintenance may originate anywhere within the software life cycle. Understanding the development phases of programs is as important as knowing how they are maintained. Both are part of the problem space.

Robert Glass and Ronald Noiseux (1981) have described the software life cycle. Their definition will provide the framework for discussing the origins of maintenance problems and the EATPUT systems used therein. Software proceeds through two general stages: it is developed and then it is maintained.

Development

Software is constructed in four stages. First, requirements and specifications are drawn up. From them a design is created. The design is converted into code. Finally, the software code and the system it is contained in are checked out; that is, the program and system are tested and verified to ensure that they satisfy the requirements and specifications of the end user. Others may interpret the development process differently, depending on the complexity of the software to be written and managerial preference. But such deviations are either expansions or contractions of the four basic steps.

Requirements and Specifications

The initial stage of development states what is expected of the proposed software. The decision to write an applied program is to solve a problem that has arisen in the end user's event world. Once the decision has been made, the next agenda item is to construct a set of requirements and specifications from which a software design can be created. What should emerge from this stage is a clear description of the output format, the input data that will be needed, the calculations that are to be performed, and any decisions that might alter the processing order. In an ideal situation an information specialist with the approval of the end user will write the requirements and specifications.

The information specialist, or whoever writes the requirements and specifications, lays the foundation upon which the remaining stages of development and maintenance rest. The demands placed on the one assigned this task are great. The specifications writer must have a thorough understanding of the development and maintenance processes, be able to quickly determine what the essential elements of the problem faced by the end user are, and have the ability to express the desires of the end user in terms that other programmers can understand. In the vocabulary of the EATPUT system:

E—the applications and computer system domain form the event world;

A—the salient features of the end user's problem space are the data that are acquired;

T—the data are transmitted to the processing component;

P—the processing component sorts through the data and stores them in an accessible form;

U—knowledge is amassed from a number of disciplines and sources to be utilized as a solution for the problem; and

T—the solution, in the form of requirements and specifications, is transferred into the event world with the approval of the end user.

Many, if not most, of the problems of maintenance can be traced to poorly written requirements and specifications. In management's eagerness to see a tangible product (i.e., code), work in the initial stages of development may be stopped prematurely or omitted. If the requirements and specifications are ambiguous, contain statements that contradict one another, or do not address portions of the end user's problem, each subsequent stage of development will be affected. It could even cause the project to be canceled. Often the programmer writing the code ends up correcting the specifications.

Design

From the specifications, a computer system is designed. At this stage, all of the processes and components necessary to develop and operate the system are described. Hardware issues, such as which computer(s) is to be used, the peripherals that will be needed, the telecommunications network that is to be employed, and so on, are determined. With respect to software, the design might include criteria for selecting a computer language to be used to write the applications program, listing or describing the software tools that will be employed in its construction, locating existing modules and programs that may be incorporated into the program, or describing all of the algorithms to be coded. For the operation of the program, the design should make known which operating system is going to be used, how the program will interface with other software, and should note any unique situations that may arise. Many of these considerations will have been decided by the hardware and software configuration in use within the software department. Those that are not will need to be described. It is important to strike a balance between overdesigning the system, which wastes money and resources, and underdesigning it, which generates errors that must be corrected later. The purpose of the design is to produce a blueprint from which the applications program can be constructed.

The EATPUT system of the software designer is different from the specification writer's system. The designer's event world is confined to the requirements and specifications and the resources used to create a computer system. Information pertinent to achieving the goals of the designer is acquired from the event world and transmitted to EATPUT components. Input data are processed into a usable form and utilized to produce a set of instructions for constructing a software product. What is transferred into the event world is the software design.

Implementation

Implementation of the design is the third stage of software development. The task of the implementation programmer is to develop a computer instruction sequence in which the solution to the end user's problem is at last realized. At the completion of this stage a tangible product will have been created.

In the programmer's event world are design documents such as decision tables, the programming language that is to be used, and the software and hardware tools necessary for writing a program. Information is acquired, transmitted, and processed as in other EATPUT systems. It will be combined with other information and knowledge, and be utilized to create the instruction sequence that will control the computer system. Constructing a program is not as straightforward as it appears. It requires considerable skill to organize and structure software that both operates efficiently and is easy to modify. A successful implementation of the design requires that the programmer pay attention to a large number of interrelationships and details. Carelessness in this regard will make the program more complex and therefore more difficult to maintain. Transferred into the event world are the software product and support documentation for the end user and maintenance programmer.

Checkout

Checkout is the last stage in software development. Its purpose is to determine whether the program satisfies the expectations of the end user. The requirements and specifications, the design, and the code are all examined. A program must be thoroughly tested and verified before it is released to the end user.

The tester's event world consists of the program, the system in which it operates, and the tools needed for validation. Many procedures will be utilized to verify that both the program and system function correctly. A good test will ensure that every requirement and specification are met, and that numerous logic combinations are tried. The tester must be diligent and patient. Error-free software transferred to the end user creates trust in both the program and the software department.

Maintenance

Maintenance is the concluding phase of the program's life cycle. How long the program will be of use to the end user depends largely on the care with which it is maintained. At this stage the responsibilities of the programmer are to adapt the program to the continually changing environments of the end user and that which occurs within the software department, and to correct errors detected in the code, the design, and the requirements and specifications. Over time, these tasks will be more difficult to achieve. At some point, the cost to maintain the program will become excessive, and it will need to be replaced or rewritten.

Alterations to programs mirror the development stages: specifications are provided via the modification request; a design is developed using the software structure in place; modifications to the sequence of instructions are written to conform to existing conventions and programming style; documentation for the end user and the maintenance programmer are updated to reflect the alterations; and the program is tested to verify that the desired change is made and that all other functions operate as intended. The primary differences from development are that each stage has already been defined and needs only to be modified, and that the scale of operation is smaller.

The maintainer may employ any or all of the EATPUT systems found in development. In small software departments, the maintainer usually does everything from helping the end user write the modification request to verifying the program and computer system. An information specialist or systems analyst may assume the responsibilities of the initial stages in large departments, leaving only the alteration of the code to the maintenance programmer.

The importance of clear unambiguous requirements and specifications and readily discernible transformations of them are most evident in the development and maintenance of large programs. Precise and accurate definitions become necessary when the duties of a programmer are restricted to a single life cycle stage, or when the turnover in programming personnel is high.

Plan of Attack

The plan of attack describes the strategy and tactics that will be employed to generate solutions for maintenance problems. Its purpose is to direct the problem-solving effort, and thereby give the project order and efficiency. The plan is designed to function within the boundaries of the approach.

Strategy

The grand strategy for solving maintenance problems is to study key elements of the problem situation, extend the definitions of those elements with the knowledge gained, and examine the problem space to see if solutions, or progress towards a solution, has been achieved. The process is to be repeated with additional studies, and will continue until the problems are resolved.

The strategy assumes that the way to produce solutions is through a more complete understanding of the problem situation. Additional knowledge of problem components increases the probability that solutions will be found.

The strategy further assumes that the problems of maintenance involve the EATPUT system of the maintainer. It is believed that problems occur in software because either the information received by the programmer was inadequate, or the maintainer's EATPUT system did not process the data that were available. What needs to be determined is, how maintainers process information, the information required for proper software maintenance, the information currently provided, and what changes can be made to enable the programmer to function more effectively.

Tactics

The plan calls for the problems of software maintenance to be attacked in a three-phase assault.

In the initial operation, the areas requiring additional understanding are identified. Topics can be attained by comparing the problem definition to the solution criteria, and noting the gaps in knowledge. The topic list should be focused and contain an assortment of items that address practical and theoretical issues.

Finding information on the topics is the second phase. The general rule is that existing knowledge is studied before new relationships are created via an experiment. Different sources, including human experts, should be considered. The preferred references are from the literature found in the library. Literature searches need to be creative and produce material that describes each subject from a number of perspectives. A subject known from many angles is more easily combined with other information and knowledge, and thereby increases the chances of finding a solution. Both applied and basic research material should be used. If the literature search fails to produce the sought-after information, an experiment can then be considered. Care needs to be taken to ensure that the information gathered is ample enough for a solution to be discovered, and yet manageable.

The last phase integrates the material collected into the problem space to see if any of the maintenance problems are now solved, or if solutions can be created from the new state.

Assimilating the new information and knowledge requires that facts and opinions be separated from theories and processes. Within each category items may be further graded into credibility classes (see Appendix H).

Using the Plan

The plan described is carried out in the remaining chapters of this book. In real situations plans are used only as a rough guide. Events usually occur in a chaotic fashion. One new discovery may cause the investigation to proceed in a different direction. Often material will be gathered merely to validate insights. What is provided is a somewhat tidy account of the process.

The research uncovered two fundamental ways to address the maintenance problems: through employing more effective symbols (Chapters 4 through 9), and by structuring the program to improve the acquisition of information and knowledge (Chapters 10 through 13).

The former is applicable to both software development and maintenance. Language is the primary means through which concepts and understandings are passed from one person to another. It is utilized by the information specialist to ascertain the desires of the end user and to create a set of specifications and requirements, and transpose them into a blueprint of a computer system. From the design, the coder employs a computer language to write the sequence of instructions for the machine. The overarching principle is that a skillfully written program is more able to withstand the many alterations that occur in maintenance than one that is casually constructed. The topics that have been researched are basic human information processing, naming things, word and letter perception, abbreviations and mnemonics, and language. The solution proposed is naming for effective maintenance (Chapter 9).

The section on structures complements the material on symbols. The principle here is that the programmer's ability to acquire, process, and utilize information can be enhanced by a well thought-out organization of the instruction sequence. That is, if software is constructed to be more compatible with the programmer's EATPUT system, it will be more easily maintained. Topics pertinent to the investigation are human problem solving, maintenance strategies and practices, and software errors and barriers to maintenance. Program and code structures for effective maintenance are presented in Chapter 13.

The testing and implementation of program changes are discussed in Chapters 14 and 15, and complete the problem-solving process. Concluding remarks are expressed in Chapter 16.

Summary

Problems in maintenance are problems with information. They will be solved by adequately meeting the information needs of the programmer.

A description of an information system is provided in Debons's EATPUT model. The system is composed of an event world where stimulation occurs, an acquisition element that senses those events, linkages between components through which messages are transmitted, a unit that processes the events acquired into existing knowledge structures, a utilization component that evaluates and applies the information towards meeting some goal, and a transfer section that interjects information into the event world.

The software life cycle consists of development and maintenance phases. The development of a program begins by describing it in terms of the end user's expectations. From the specifications an information system is drafted, and then implemented as computer code. Development is complete when the code has been checked out against the requirements.

In the literature, program maintenance is categorized as adaptive, perfective, or corrective. The first two adapt software to the changing environments of the end user and the software department, respectively. They consume most of the maintenance resources. The process of maintaining software is similar to development, differing mainly in scale.

The plan of attack to solve maintenance problems consists of three phases. In the initial phase, areas are identified where additional understanding is needed. Information is gathered on the topics in the next phase. And lastly, the material is assembled in a meaningful whole and applied to the problem.

Section II
Solutions Through Symbols

Chapter 4
Some Basics

Problems, like the ones found in software maintenance, are best resolved through a clear and fundamental understanding of their underlying causes. Common sense tells us that programmers who are able to readily comprehend the function of computer code and are able to quickly locate a desired program segment will have a decided edge over those who cannot. They will not only be able to complete maintenance tasks sooner, but will also perform them more accurately. Knowing some basics of how the mind, or long-term memory, operates lays the foundation upon which that understanding is able to be constructed.

Although the mind has been extensively studied, how it processes and utilizes information is not precisely known (Pylyshyn, 1984). From the natural sciences we have gained knowledge about axioms, synapses, and the anatomic structure of the brain. But we do not know specifically how our experiences are encoded and how they are used to evoke abstract thought. From cognitive psychology and linguistics we know a good deal about symbols (i.e., words), and how they combine to form sentences (Hayakawa, 1941; Chomsky, 1972; Miller & Johnson-Laird, 1976; Dowty, 1979; Winograd, 1983). What we do not yet understand is what symbols are attached to and how that component is affected when symbols are strung together into meaningful phrases and paragraphs. Stated in other words, we know a lot about the neurological structure, and a lot about symbol relationships, but not much about how the two interconnect. Although our understanding of the mind may be incomplete, insights into its operation can still be achieved by studying human reactions to sensory input, observing how symbols are used and interpreted, and examining the processes of recognition and recall of events in memory. Symbol usage is a particular type of communication with another.[4] Programmers who know how to effectively use symbols to represent concepts will be able to write software that is easier to maintain.

In the mind there are three distinct functional areas: procedural, semantic, and episodic memories. Each component of long-term memory processes and utilizes information differently.

---

[4] Although graphic and hypertext programs make extensive use of sensory information, software is primarily written and maintained through symbols.

Procedural Memory

Procedural memory forms the base of a three-tiered hierarchy that describes long-term memory. From it extends a specialized subsystem called semantic memory. Episodic memory is at the top level, and functions as a specialized subsystem of semantic memory. Each memory is dependent on the level(s) below it. Only procedural memory can act alone (Tulving, 1985).

Procedural memory is used to attain goals. Housed in it are event sequences that control the muscle activity in the arm for throwing a baseball, and that enable a programmer to sift through a bewildering array of data to correct an error in a section of code. Its information is prescriptive, and does not need descriptions of the event world or an account of the individual's personal history to operate. Its purpose is to diagram a course of action to be taken (Tulving, 1985).

Processing

When an individual responds in specific ways to specific stimuli, the connections are processed in procedural memory. Causal associations that are new are recorded as they were originally encountered. As responses are repeatedly linked with the same stimuli, their bonds are strengthened. Learning occurs "nonknowingly" through tuning (Tulving, 1985).

What structure the information is processed into cannot be precisely determined. One model, proposed by Roger Schank (1980), views it as a mixture of causal and inferred information. In it are two levels of causal chains: a micro level that organizes primitive events and a macro level that causally links together information and is more general. Four hierarchical levels of information enable the memory to interact with the event world. Each level is resilient, and is able to infer certain items that are missing. At the first level are scripts. They assemble causal chains into basic units of belief and knowledge, and link together world events that would not typically be connected based on their superficial attributes. Causal chains may not always possess enough detail to bring some events into contact with each other. Through scripts, those associations are possible. Scripts have the ability to infer missing chains and the script in use. The selection of a script is made at the next level dealing with plans. Plans are principally concerned with the motivations and intentions of some intelligent being or artifact. They are selected to pursue goals, and are able to infer the plan in use and the present goal to be achieved. Goal issues are addressed at the next higher level. Here it is determined which goals are in conflict, which can be subsumed, what other goals can be inferred, and the extent of their applicability. The highest level makes inferences about themes. It ascertains which themes are likely to be present, which are compatible, and which need their differences resolved.

In programming, software maintenance is an example of a theme. Within the theme, one goal would be to understand a section of code. Defining the functions performed within the section and determining their significance within the program illustrates a plan used to achieve that goal. Scripts bring together the variables and processes that compose a function. They assemble causal linkages, in the forms of lines of code (macro level) and symbols (micro level) that represent computer operations and the names given to variables, files, and routines, into a meaningful unit. Procedural memory directs the problem-solving process.

Utilization

The individual utilizes procedural memory to make overt intelligent responses to external and internal stimuli (Tulving, 1985; Mitchell, 1989). The information is accessed according to how it was encoded, and is employed, for example, to complete word fragments and stems, in lexical descriptions, and in associative priming (Mitchell, 1989).

Procedural memory is used by the maintenance programmer to solve problems, plan, and understand the mnemonic names given to routines, files, and variables.

Semantic Memory

Semantic memory records our knowledge of the event world. In it are housed mental representations of objects, actions, and other concepts that we may have. It acts as a repository for things that can be described (Tulving, 1985, 1993; Mitchell, 1989).

Semantic memory is what gives us a "knowing" consciousness. It enables us to have abstract thought and to perform mental operations on concepts we extract from our external and internal worlds. Things initially experienced via the senses can be stored here and later recalled (Tulving, 1985, 1993; Mitchell, 1989).

Processing

Semantic memory processes information primarily by making associations among symbols, lists, and rules (Simon, 1969). These associations determine whether information will be used to reinforce established structures or bring into existence new symbols and relationships. Symbol processing includes attaching symbols to concepts, grouping symbols into lists, relating symbols through the use of a rule, and activating existing relationships (Bower, 1970). When the semantic system is restructured, learning is achieved (Tulving, 1985).

Examples of symbols are the names given to computer files, programs, and variables. They are attached to either a concept or another symbol. Symbols are not randomly distributed. Those having similar meanings, or that become related through a function, are clustered into units called memory organization packets (MOPs) or chunks (Schank, 1980; Bellezza & Young, 1989). A MOP may be either a list or a rule (Bower, 1970). The former is an array of symbols having a common attribute (e.g., a list of sort routines may have as its members alphabetic, binary, bubble, etc.). The latter describes a process in which two or more symbols are brought into temporary association. For example, an arithmetic statement establishes a relationship among certain variables in a program (e.g., $X = Y + Z$). Rules are what enable abstract thought (Bower, 1970).

Utilization

Access to information in semantic memory is not constrained by a stimulus-response structure. Information created in one situation may be utilized in a context that is entirely different, and exhibit a behavior that is unlike the one originally learned (Tulving, 1985). Flexible use of information is a trait characteristic of semantic memory.

The act of bringing information into an active state is called retrieval. It is achieved through recognition and recall.

Recognition means simply that a symbol in conscious memory is acknowledged to have been processed before. It is accompanied by its meaning, but its relationship to other symbols and its role within the global structure are not revealed. For example, if we see the word sort in a program, we are aware of what it does, but we do not necessarily know how it functions in a program.

Recall brings concepts and symbols into awareness. The internal order of the symbols to be activated does not matter. Items that are grouped together receive the same stimulation (Bower, 1970).

The recall of information can be directed through the use of cues, if procedural memory is utilized. Cues are symbols and must be associated with the target in some way. Such connections are formed, for example, in a repetitive learning situation. Note that how items are organized in procedural memory has a direct bearing on how they will be later recalled. In a repetitive learning situation, consistency of the first term in a group will facilitate recall (Bower, 1970; Reber & Lewis, 1977; Reber & Allen, 1978). If an individual is presented data that are inconsistent with the internal structure, learning will be impaired (Reber, 1969; Bower, 1970; Jones cited in Reber & Lewis, 1977; Young & Bellezza, 1982).

Semantic memory is typically depicted as a network consisting of an array of nodes representing objects, properties, and categories. Each node is connected to other nodes by a directed line representing a relationship. Extracting the portions of relationships that sufficiently describe the referents creates definitions. For example, the definition of "dog" would include links to the general categories of mammal and pet, and to such characteristics as barking and having fur (Miller & Charles, 1991).

Understanding the meaning of sentences and lines of code is a complex process because much of what we say and write has conceptual dependency (Schank, 1980). The process uses conceptual rules, reflecting an "interlingual meaning structure," in conjunction with rules or grammar to provide the individual with the missing concepts of an expression. Directing the person towards a thought completion are expectations created in social discourse. To illustrate, consider the following situation. You are in New York City, desiring to go to John F. Kennedy Airport. What do you do? You take your luggage to the edge of the sidewalk, hail a taxi, and ask the driver to take you to Kennedy. No additional elaborations are necessary. The omitted components of the name are implied, and are subconsciously attached, in procedural memory, to the name stem because of past encounters with Kennedy and luggage and airport and other referents. These relationships or conceptual rules comprise in part its interlingual meaning structure. Ignoring or misinterpreting the interlingual meaning structure of the end user and maintainer is a common error in programming.

Episodic Memory

Episodic memory stores our personal experiences. Every time we see the sun set behind a range of mountains, talk on the telephone with our best friend, or visit the dentist to have a cavity filled, processing of some kind will occur in episodic memory. Episodic memory gives us our identity. It orients the individual in time and space. With it we have the capacity for experiencing past events and imagining future situations. Episodic memory is our "self-knowing" consciousness (Tulving, 1985, 1993).

Processing

Events registered in episodic memory may originate from cognitive activity or from observations of the external world. Each event accretes within memory in a form isomorphic to what it represents. This is how learning is achieved (Tulving, 1985).

To illustrate how events may be processed in episodic memory, consider the function of a memory model composed of four levels of abstraction. At its most primitive level is "event memory," where the details of a particular experience are stored. At each succeeding level, the information is more general. During processing, our perceptions of an episode enter memory and in a short time decay. Only those making an impact will remain. Features common to many experiences become abstract in form, and are part of "general event memory." In processing, this information is made available to event memory. A link connecting the memories is established and the initial information fades. What remains about the episode are references to general event memory and any residual features of note. In like manner, items in general event memory point to the more abstract information in "situation memory." Stored here are descriptions of specific scenes, the rules governing them, and definitions of typical experiences. During cognition, they are used to bring contextual relevance to situations. "Intentional memory" is the most general level of abstraction. It contains the rules for plan and goal achievement (Schank, 1980).

Episodic memory seems to have an unlimited capacity for storing concepts. It must also have the ability to automatically associate events having similar characteristics and be able to recall portions of past events that apply to present situations (Richards, 1988).

Utilization

Episodic memory is used for recalling experiences and imagining future situations. It is characterized by the same flexible access to information that exists in semantic memory (Tulving, 1985).

Information specialists, systems analysts, and coders employ episodic memory to construct information systems for the end user that programmers can maintain. They also draw on past experiences to recall the problems and the techniques that worked in situations similar to ones in which software will be embedded.

Summary

Long-term memory is divided into procedural, semantic, and episodic areas. These areas are structured as a hierarchy, with procedural memory forming the base, semantic memory extending from it as a special subsystem, and episodic memory protruding from semantic memory in a similar way.

Procedural memory is a collection of stimulus-response assemblies, containing information about plans and goals. The items contained in it are rigidly fixed in their original storage form. Procedural memory is "nonknowing" memory (Allen & Reber, 1980).

Semantic memory is "knowing" memory. It houses our knowledge of the world. Things that can be defined are stored there. Semantic and episodic memories are characterized by a flexible storage structure.

Episodic memory enables us to recall past events and envision future situations. It is "self-knowing" memory.

The conscious mind (i.e., semantic and episodic memories) is an elaborate collection of items that are able to freely combine with each other. It functions by progressing from one thought to another by a process called spreading activation (Richards, 1988; Ratcliff & McKoon, 1988; Yantis & Meyer, 1988). An item brought into consciousness will cue an associated item, bringing that item into awareness, that item will activate others, and so forth. Preventing the entire memory from being accessed is a series of constraints that are also processed at that time. They serve to restrict the extent of activation, and direct it along a purposeful path.

Chapter 5
Naming

Software maintainers learn the functions of programs primarily through their code. Aiding programmers in this pursuit are the names given to variables, routines, and files.

For this reason, understanding the naming process is important for all members of the programming community. Software designers must know the principles underlying the process to develop naming systems that evoke appropriate concepts and that can be extended to include names for additional referents. Maintainers need such knowledge to readily comprehend the intent of the originator of the computer term and to enhance the capabilities of the program in accordance with existing conventions. Researchers have to be aware of the process to address the naming issues that arise in applications software and programming languages.

The EATPUT system serves as a model for the naming process. From that knowledge, systems of names may be analyzed. Names are studied in the context of the referent and how they relate to other names in semantic memory.

The Naming Process

Names are symbols used to represent objects and events. Their selection is based on the perception of the referent and is influenced by the context in which the referent is found, the cognitive state of the namer, and the audience to which the name is directed. The process occurs within the individual or through social interaction.

Event World

The naming process begins when an individual or group desires to retain the thought of an object or event for later reference. The referent is identified along with its context. The latter is often incorporated into the name (e.g., sea horse, mountain lion, water polo, etc.).

Acquisition

In acquisition mode, some distinguishing aspect of the referent is captured for retention. What that might be depends on the perceptual predisposition of the individual. Primarily it is the goals and objectives pursued by the namer that determine the type and degree of involvement he has with the referent and the trait captured. If the namer is actively engaged with the referent on a continuing basis, he will more likely extract concrete traits than when his association is passive and the situation temporary (Carroll, 1980b). Therefore, program artifacts named by maintainers should be pertinent to their tasks, and ones provided by others less appropriate.

Transmission

Information is passed from one EATPUT component to another.

Processing

In processing, the trait captured to represent the referent is attached to a symbol, and the name along with its meaning becomes part of semantic memory. Which part of speech the name assumes depends on the trait extracted. For objects, the name selected is typically a simple noun (Carroll, 1980b, 1981). However, if the referent is novel, additional information may be needed to identify it, and a compound name frequently will be used (Carroll, 1981). References to procedures take names from verb phrases. Those traits that reflect the roles the referent plays in the event world obtain names from adjective phrases (Carroll, 1981).

In general, programmers are typically concerned with solving only the problem at hand and give inadequate attention to the effects their names will have on others.

Utilization and Transfer

Using the name in the event world completes the naming process for an individual. But when a group performs the process, there will be many preliminary transfers of information before the symbol is offered to a larger community.

Names created in a social environment are better suited to function within a given community than ones typically proffered by a lone individual. Their acceptance is based on their utility within the cognitive states of a number of people, as opposed to just one individual. However, before name acceptance takes place, the community must decide on a common goal, value, and belief structure, and a context, or set of contrasting alternatives, in which the referent is to be compared. Agreement on this communal cognitive state and context is negotiated tacitly. Seldom are any of the details of the naming process overtly discussed. Communicators simply exchange descriptions of the referent. As each becomes familiar with the exchanges of the other(s), the descriptions become shortened. That is, as the parties involved in the naming process arrive at a common cognitive state and context, and as the referent becomes contextually dependent among existing structures, the words needed to convey what is meant become fewer. Eventually a name is suggested by one of the participants, and is accepted by the other(s). Rarely is there a progressive exchange of descriptive pruning. The arrived-at name usually appears as the dominant context word in the initial descriptions, and seems to pop out in the course of dialogue (Carroll, 1980c). Thus, once the referent's conceptual dependencies are explored, the symbol evoking the most useful information is selected to represent it. Naming is a shortening process (see Appendix I).

Names of software artifacts should be created for use in maintenance. There are many goals competing for primacy in the naming process: descriptiveness, brevity, uniqueness, culture, and the like. Naming is essentially a compromise in achieving these desired ends (Carroll, 1981).

Analyzing Names

Names may be analyzed in two fundamental ways. They can be studied in the context in which they were created, and according to their relationships to other symbols in semantic memory.

Names in Context

Names and words attain meaning from the contexts in which they are used. Meanings are not represented internally by pictures of referents, but as contrasts of referents among minimal sets of distinguishing alternates.[5] Because referents can always be placed against different sets of descriptors, the possibility for new perceptions are endless. Meanings specify not only what referents are, but what they are not. They both reduce uncertainty and reflect the individual's partitioning of the event world.

To illustrate, suppose a person is asked to provide a name for a white ball placed between a blue pyramid and a red cube. By responding "ball" the request is satisfied. If the composition of the set is altered to be a blue ball, a red ball, and a white ball, the same reply will not identify the object. Now another attribute, such as color, must be used to avoid ambiguity. With a set of three identical white balls, the position of the referent in the set would be used to distinguish one white ball from the others. The point is that as the context is changed, the attibute(s) uniquely representing the symbol-referent pairs may also need to be reexamined (Olson, 1970; Carroll, 1980a, 1980b, 1981).

---

[5] The amount of storage space required for an extensive library of referent pictures, and the time required to sort through such a library and retrieve a desired image, exceeds the physical limitations of the brain and memory (Olson, 1970).

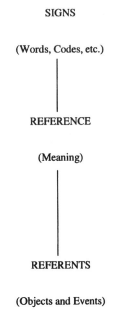

SIGNS

(Words, Codes, etc.)

REFERENCE

(Meaning)

REFERENTS

(Objects and Events)

Figure 4. Ogden and Richards's Basic Reference Modal. From "Language and Thought: Aspects of a Cognitive Theory of Semantics" by D. R. Olson, 1970, *Psychological Review*, 77(4). Copyright 1970 by the American Psychological Association. Adapted by permission.

Care must be taken when naming to ensure that the symbol-reference-referent relationship best reflects its application within the user's environment. A little foresight will help reduce meaning drift and guard against naming referents in one environment but using them in another.

Meaning drift occurs because different objects and events keep entering our awareness and form new contexts, and because long-term memory is continually being modified through the routine processing of information (Miller & Charles, 1991). As goals are achieved, they are replaced by new ones, and plans and values are updated. The new processing configuration causes other objects to be observed and focuses the attention on different levels of detail. In a fine-grained analysis, a word will have meaning for only a limited amount of time because the context is intact only briefly. But in that short time it will have altered the internal representation of the referent. Interactions with the event world produce a corresponding change in the cognitive state.

The names found in software are rarely created with the maintainer and his tasks in mind. The developers who attach symbols to referents operate under a set of goals and criteria that are not entirely consistent with those of maintenance. Information specialists need to use the experiences of maintainers and employ episodic memory to conjure up maintenance scenarios from which to name referents.

Words in Semantic Memory

As we employ words to express our thoughts and desires as they are used in social discourse to achieve our ends, they become incorporated into semantic memory. The internal relationships they form vary. Words become linked when they refer to the same things (e.g., cat and feline) or have similar meanings within a common contextual boundary (Miller & Charles, 1991). If certain objects perform related functions in the same scenario, the words representing them will be grouped together (e.g., a knife, fork, spoon, napkin, and plate form a place setting within a dining situation). Words having opposite meanings are paired. Antonyms may be further categorized as: "contradictory terms (perfect/imperfect), contrary terms (white/black), reverse terms (constructive/destructive), contrasted terms (rich/destitute), incompatible or loosely contrasted terms (frank/hypocritical), relative terms (parent/child), and complementary terms (question/answer)" (Egan cited in Gross, Fischer, & Miller, 1989). Associated with each antonym pair is an adjective cluster of similar meanings (Gross, Fischer, & Miller, 1989). Words also may be organized into relational hierarchies (e.g., leopard, cat, animal, mammal, and thing). It is from these relationships that new words are formed and analyzed (Gross, Fischer, & Miller, 1989).

One method used to analyze words is to study them from common prefix, stem, and suffix units or rule-schemes (Carroll, 1980c, 1981, 1983). From these groupings, names for new referents are suggested. For example, "mean age," "mean height," and "mean weight" have the rule-scheme "mean____," and infer that the name for mean average income is "mean income."

Another technique is to plot a rule-scheme or name set from some namespace (N) against the attributes referenced by the names in some reference-space (R) to determine if the array is isomorphic or congruent. Names are isomorphic when there is a one-to-one mapping between the spaces. Congruence occurs if the names are both isomorphic and maintain the ordinal nominal distance in the R-space. The nominal distance relationship is a measure of the number of dimensions in which the referents differ. The fewer dimensions there are that differ, the shorter the distance is. Names and words that vary with their referents along one dimension are more congruent than those that change along two. An example of congruence is shown in Figures 5 and 6, depicting a light switch. The switch has two dimensions. One refers to its electrical state (on or off). The other reflects the physical state (up or down) (Carroll, 1980d).

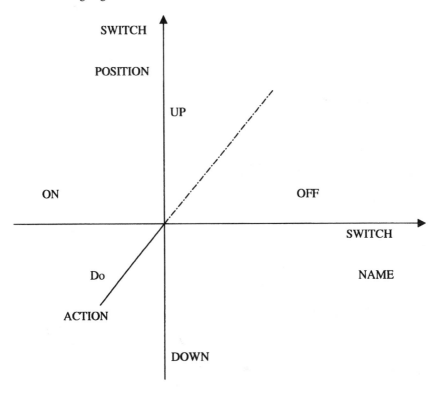

Figure 5. Simple R-Space for the Control Switch Domain. From "Naming as a Mapping Between N-Dimensional Geometries" by J. M. Carroll, 1980d, *IBM Research Report*, RC 8596 (#37275).

The names used in software need to be clear, precise, and unambiguous. They must evoke their intended meaning, without confusing the programmer by bringing to mind competing thoughts. Popular names have a one-to-many mapping and require other words or a context to filter out unwanted referents. Words that are employed infrequently are more congruent. They have not been exposed to as many contexts and therefore have not been as extensively modified (Charles & Miller, 1989). Their meanings have remained limited whereas the more popular words have expanded (Black & Moran, 1981; Barnard et al., 1981; Rosenberg, 1981, 1983; Landauer, Galotti, & Hartwell, 1983; Grudin & Barnard, 1984).

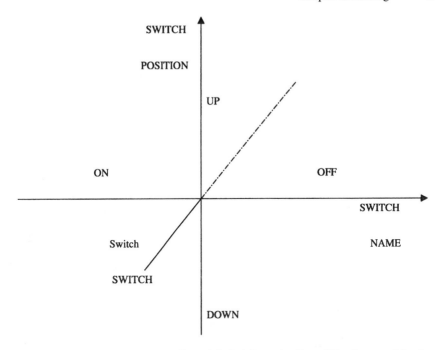

Figure 6. Simple N-Space for the Control Switch Domain. From "Naming as a Mapping Between N-Dimensional Geometries" by J. M. Carroll, 1980d, *IBM Research Report*, RC 8596 (#37275).

The effects of word popularity can be seen in a class of naming conventions known as command names.[6] When popular words, such as "alter" and "correct," are used as commands, the end user must choose the appropriate meaning to employ from a number of alternates. The commands "insert" and "delete," on the other hand, are words that are infrequently used. These commands and their meanings are more congruent, and hence are readily understood and quickly learned. The features of command names should closely match the actions or operations they represent (Rosenberg, 1981). As components of a naming convention, command names should reflect an implicit model of the name-action relationships. The degree of appropriateness of command names is the degree to which the names are isomorphic to the actions they evoke, and the degree to which the names suggest other names in the system (Barnard et al., 1981).

---

[6] Command names refer to the set of words made available to the end user for controlling the operation of the program.

Summary

Knowledge of the naming process provides a basis for developing more effective representations for variables, routines, and files, and leads to a better understanding of the code.

There are many factors competing for dominance within the naming process. A few of these are context, involvement with the referent, and the intended audience. Names for personal use are casually given and may reflect the unique experiences of the individual. Names developed within a group must function within a common context and a communal cognitive state. Such an agreement is accomplished tacitly through an exchange of referent descriptions. Initially the referent is fully described. As agreement to context and cognitive state materialize, the descriptions become shortened. Eventually a name emerges, and is accepted by the group.

Names are analyzed in the context of the referents and how they relate to other names in semantic memory. With respect to context, the symbol chosen denotes a feature that distinguishes the referent from the others within a minimal set of contrasting alternates. Often the context is incorporated into the name. Names are also studied from the relationships they form with other names and words. A desired feature of name sets is congruence. Names and words are congruent if there is a one-to-one mapping between the names and referents, and if ordinal nominal distance relationship is retained among the names and referents. Congruent names are desired because they convey precise unambiguous meanings.

Chapter 6
Words and Letters

Whether programming names are letter strings in procedural memory or words in semantic memory has a profound impact on the quality of software. Word and letter relationships help determine how names will be interpreted and learned. Understanding them, and the memories in which they are used, provides a basis from which existing software nomenclature can be better discerned and names can be abbreviated to form useful mnemonics.

The chapter steps through topics relevant to software maintenance in the initial two levels of memory. It begins with Symbols in Procedural Memory, and addresses situations often encountered in legacy software. Procedural and Semantic Memory Interaction lays the foundation for improving word abbreviations and mnemonics. Covered in Symbols in Semantic Memory are word recognition and recall. Other Factors in Word Retrieval lists additional aspects of using semantic networks.

Symbols in Procedural Memory

When programmers run across names they do not understand, the symbol strings representing the variables, routines, and files are processed in procedural memory. They make up the data-driven portion of the knowledge spectrum and do not evoke concepts. Maintainers frequently see them during work on legacy software.

Learning Processing Operations

Learning data-driven naming conventions is similar to learning miniature artificial languages (MAL; see Appendix J). Acquisition is attained through two processes. One records the relational consistencies in character strings. In general, frequently seen character pairs are learned first and the less salient combinations later. Placement of the pair within the word affects acquisition. Pairs in the first positions are captured the quickest, followed by ones in the end positions. Internal pairs are obtained last. The other operation assesses the entire word or MAL sentence for its adherence to the permissible rules of association (Reber & Lewis, 1977).

Acquisition

How quickly and thoroughly a naming convention is learned depends on the complexity of the rule and formulation assembly used to generate the symbol network in procedural memory, and the processes used to attain it. The means of acquisition can be explicit (e.g., learning rules and formulations from definitions), implicit (e.g., acquiring nonconscious knowledge of symbol pairings through observation), or a combination of the two (Reber & Lewis, 1977; Reber et al., 1980; Reber, Allen, & Regan, 1985).

For small programs and those in which the rule and formulation structure are simple, it is easier to explicitly learn definitions. Committing a few rules to memory does require a small investment of time. However, once learned, the rule set can be used to help spot mislabeled variables and suggest new representations for use in the routine. Learning the rule set implicitly would take longer and is prone to error (Reber & Allen, 1978).

When the rule structure is complex, an explicit learning strategy becomes impractical. There are too many rules to acquire and put to use. A more effective method to employ is implicit learning. Implicit learning is a natural, although unconscious, process. Rules can be obtained when either a small subset (25%) of the examples has been seen a number of times, or a large subset is viewed only a few times (Palermo & Parrish, 1971; Nagata, 1976).

Learning Factors

The strategies used to discover the regularities in symbol strings are affected by their role within the task to be performed, the environment in which they are used, and the complexity of the strings themselves. These factors also determine whether the rules of grammar will be abstracted into implicit rules or left as isolated events (McLaughlin, 1981). When a set of MAL character strings is observed in the absence of a particular goal or purpose, the rules of grammar will be acquired by inducing them from usages in the names of variables, routines, and files. These abstract representations are then employed to determine if novel letter strings conform to the rules of association. A rule induction strategy however can be replaced by an analogic one, if the means of learning are altered (Reber & Allen, 1978). That will happen if the programmer associates the letters in a variable name to a mnemonic device for later recall.

Another factor influencing learning is personal outlook. Belief in one's ability to affect change determines how symbols are organized in procedural memory. People believing that events are unaffected by their behavior are "externals." Those that do are called "internals." Internals feel that their actions control events, and tend to organize information for recall more effectively than externals. They are also more prone to seek control information, and acquire a better understanding of the underlying grammar (Kassin & Reber, 1979).

Procedural and Semantic Memory Interaction

The letters and orthogonal fragments contained in procedural memory are used to compose the names, words, and word fragments of semantic memory. When symbols become attached to meaning components, they receive stimuli from both memories, and are remembered better than either orthogonal fragments or random characters.

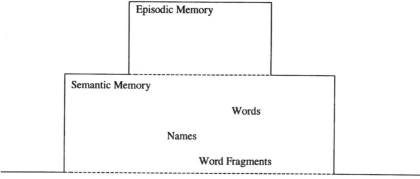

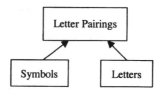

Figure 7. General Word-Letter Model.

Symbols and thoughts propagate through and between the memories by a process called spreading activation. When we read, the words we see evoke thoughts. Those stimulate other thoughts and words related to them in some way, and those still others. Influencing what we read are our present cognitive state and perception of the event world. They combine to create expectations for certain words. To communicate our thoughts to others, words are retrieved from semantic memory and assembled in a form that expresses them. What manages the process, accessing the memories needed and controlling spreading activation is the focus of attention (Koriat & Melkman, 1987).

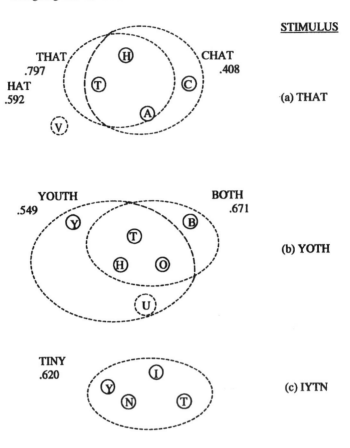

Figure 8. Schematic of the Associative Lexical Network. From "Models of Word Recognition" by M. J. Adams, 1979, *Cognitive Psychology*, 11.

Maintainers determine what the originator of the code meant, largely from the abbreviated names given to variables, routines, and files. If the mnemonics are well constructed, the programmer will readily be able to fill in the missing characters and interpret the expression as intended. For example, when reading the variable "AVETIM," each letter is first processed as a single unit, and then becomes paired according to the strength of its probability of association. These causal relationships in procedural memory follow the spelling rules the individual has acquired through years of reading and study. Several orthogonal pairs will be recognized ("AV," "VE," "ET," "TI," etc.), and in turn will stimulate words in semantic memory. With the event world creating expectations for certain words, the maintainer will easily conclude that the name is "average time." Word recognition and recall are affected by an interfacilitating force within memory (Wheeler, 1970; Richards & Heller, 1979; Adams, 1979; Tweedy & Lapinski, 1981; Perlman, 1984; den Heyer, 1985).

Symbols in Semantic Memory

Symbols in semantic memory define the event world, and are used by all members of the software community. They comprise the cognitive-driven portion of the knowledge spectrum. Programmers refer to them through abbreviations and mnemonics. Information specialists and systems analysts use them when creating names for variables, routines, and files. Understanding how words are recognized, and knowing their characteristics and the relationships they form lead to more coherent programming.

Recognizing Words

Words are processed in a manner similar to letter strings in procedural memory. They are recognized if they can be matched to internal representations. Comparisons are made either by matching the first syllables of the word, or by a one-to-one mapping of component letters (Chambers, 1979).

Comparison methods differ according to the length of the word encountered. For short words, a match of the individual letters is used. All letters must agree. A discrepancy of a single character will prevent recognition. However, transposition of interior letter pairs of high frequency words will not (Chambers, 1979).

The first syllable stems are used to recognize long words. Internal representations are accessed by matching all of the prefix syllables and the first syllable stem. The last syllable may also contribute to word recognition, but to a far lesser degree (Taft & Forster, 1976).

Recalling Words

Certain activities within the mind prime words for recognition and recall. One is context. Words that are conceptually related, or are used in a particular situation, are stimulated to a degree when that context is used. Words are also primed if they bear a semantic kinship to a symbol in an active state (Marohn & Hochhaus, 1988). A thought evoked by one symbol will in turn activate other symbols that represent it in some way. The words that receive the most priming are the most familiar. They are the ones used in many contexts and are connected to a large symbol array (Tweedy & Lapinski, 1981; Miller, 1981; den Heyer, 1985). Selecting a vocabulary germane to the software environment produces a more understandable program.

Whether a word enters into conscious thought depends on its relative strength of association with the symbols presently active. The candidate has to amass an association strength exceeding the threshold created by the established set (Nelson et al., 1989). Success need not depend solely on the symbol's own association strength. Several lexical items may combine to activate a word that would not be brought into consciousness otherwise (Duffy, Henderson, & Morris, 1989). These combinations develop through a process independent of the one that determines the overall meaning of a sentence or line of code (Masson, 1988; MacLeod, 1989).

The set of words and thoughts in the conscious state are modified when sentences and lines of code are read, and through other mental activity. Through reading, new items are brought into consciousness, causing some word associations to be strengthened and making other words fall out of awareness by redirecting the focus of attention to some other concern (Rosenberg, 1987). Words activated through mental activity are more distinct than those from reading. They were created from a contrast with similar internal representations, and have an advantage in subsequent attempts at recognition and recall.

Words failing in their bid for awareness retain their potential and may be activated in a later attempt. These words are superadditive. However, if the basis for retrieval is for an inappropriate reason, such as mass repetition, they will be subadditive (Begg & Green, 1988).

Other Factors in Word Retrieval

There are other factors to consider when selecting words for programming names. It is particularly important to be aware of symbol relationships in semantic memory and how words may be interpreted in the event world.

Degrees of Abstraction

The word's degree of abstraction is a measure of its representativeness. The more abstract a word is, the more it relies on context and additional information for comprehension.

Concrete words are usually recognized more readily than abstract ones (Schwanenflugel & Stowe, 1989).

Word Fragments

Word fragments are used frequently in software as mnemonic devices. Programmers recognize them if a search of the lexical entries in semantic memory produces a match. The search does not depend on retrieving encoded meanings (Nelson, Keelean, & Negrao, 1989).

Word fragments that require additional processing to recall a referent can be more effective than complete words (Johns & Swanson, 1988; Gardiner, Gregg, & Hampton, 1988; Begg et al., 1989).

"Neighborhood Effect"

Words do not enter conscious thought unaffected by their networks of association. Words related to them help to determine their use and how they will be recognized and recalled. This is the "neighborhood effect." Whether it will be a positive or negative factor depends on the word's frequency of usage. For low frequency words a large cluster of relationships facilitates retrieval. The opposite is true for high frequency words (Andrews, 1989).

Word Use

The memory a word is used in affects its retrieval. For episodic tasks, infrequently used words outperform those more often employed (Mutter & Hashtroudi, 1987). High frequency words are better in lexical decisions (Duchek & Neely, 1989).

Summary

When programmers encounter names they do not understand, the symbol strings representing the variables, routines, and files are processed in procedural memory. Symbols in procedural memory are data driven and do not evoke concepts. Maintainers often see them in legacy software.

For procedural symbol strings, letter pairs in the first positions are learned first, those in the last positions next, then internal pairs. Learning the rule structure governing letter associations prior to viewing a large program produces better results than relying on implicit acquisition.

The interaction between procedural and semantic memories is dynamic. Symbols and thoughts propagate through the memories by spreading activation. Controlling the activity is the focus of attention.

Symbols in semantic memory define the event world, and are used by all members of the software community. They comprise the cognitive-driven portion of the knowledge spectrum.

Semantic words are processed like symbol strings in procedural memory.

Context and semantic kinship prime words for retrieval.

Chapter 7
Abbreviations and Mnemonics

Abbreviating words into useful mnemonic names has been a primary concern of programmers from the earliest days of computing. There are many abbreviating schemes about, and each programmer seems to have a favorite. However, processes are only as effective as the tenets upon which they are built. Methods that are not well thought out and principled are not able to handle the stream of coding alterations that occur during maintenance.

In this chapter, the basic principles of abbreviating and creating mnemonics in software are introduced. The initial two sections discuss what abbreviations and mnemonics are, their utility, and their general properties. Next, the basic techniques for shortening words are defined. Their performances are then assessed and compared in the different tasks and situations occurring in maintenance.

Abbreviations

Because of the ease with which they can be communicated, abbreviated names are widely used in both the written and oral modes (Carroll, 1982; Gabriele & Frauenhofer, 1984). Name abbreviation occurs naturally (Zipf cited in Streeter, Ackroff, & Taylor, 1983) as a continuation of a shortening process. When words are frequently used, more about the term becomes incorporated into the memory structure, and less information needs to be conveyed to the reader or listener. For example, the once frequently used word "condominium" is now "condo." Sometimes the referent becomes so strongly associated with the abbreviation that the antecedent word is obscured (e.g., p. m. is used instead of post meridiem). Abbreviating names is an accepted practice, and is necessary for effective communications.

Mnemonics

The purpose of mnemonics is to assist the programmer in determining the function or contents of variables, routines, and files. The degree to which that end is achieved depends largely on the size of the program, the software's complexity, the appropriateness of the antecedent name, and the abbreviation technique used. For small straightforward programs, mnemonics contribute little toward program understanding. Variable contents and the function of code segments are apparent. As programs increase in size and complexity, variable definitions and the interrelationships among software components become less obvious, and the role of mnemonics grows in significance (Sheppard et al., 1979; Sheil, 1981; Shneiderman, 1980).

When properly constructed, mnemonics convey useful information about the program to the maintainer. That is, program entities are adequately described, the most effective mnemonic technique is employed, and the maintainer is able to interpret the code and receive its intended message. Names that are ill-conceived add to software complexity (Von Wright, 1970; Shneiderman, 1980).

Abbreviating names to useful mnemonics occurs naturally. When making entries on a patient's medical chart, physicians shorten terms to three or four characters, and frequently to a single letter (Gabriele & Frauenhofer, 1984). Computer users, given the opportunity, abbreviate names to fewer than six characters (Benbasat, Dexter, & Masulis, 1981).

Whether it is a user interface or a coding convention, learning a system of mnemonics and referents takes time. Problems may arise in situations where the full name is naturally recalled. This happens when users having little familiarity with a system try to recall a command for a sought-after response. It also occurs as programmers, not acquainted with the naming convention in use, attempt to name variables. If the full name of a command or variable is recalled, any additional requirement to transform it to an abbreviation only increases the internal processing to be done (Grudin & Barnard, 1984). The issue is of particular interest to programmers designing command name schemes and to those using a compiler language, such as COBOL, that permits the use of longer variable names. To lessen the impact, names should be selected for their ability to best represent the desired response, and the abbreviation technique used should require little translation. With use, the mnemonic will become more strongly associated with the referent, and the problem will disappear.

Basic Techniques

There are many different abbreviation strategies used by programmers. Although large in number, the abbreviation schemes typically encountered can be created from combinations of only four basic methods: truncation, contraction, phonics, and concatenation.

Truncation

Truncation shortens full words by deleting one or more of the name's trailing letters. To be effective, the resultant word stem will contain enough visual cues for the maintainer to recall the complete name (Rogers & Moeller, 1984). Truncation is particularly well suited for abbreviating multisyllable words (Taft & Forster, 1976; Streeter, Ackroff, & Taylor, 1983), and is often used in combination with other methods.

Words may be truncated by retaining a fixed number of initial letters or by using the fewest initial letters that will distinguish it from the other abbreviations in the system. In the former, a fixed length of six letters will produce the abbreviations SUBSTI, SUBTRA, and STORED from the command names SUBSTITUTE, SUBTRACT, and STORE DATA. The latter abbreviates these names to SUBS, SUBT, and ST.

Contraction

Contraction abbreviates a word by striking out one or more of its internal letters. With this method, the commands CHANGE, ALTER, and MODIFY become CHG, ALTR, and MDFY. The last two mnemonics illustrate a special category of contraction called vowel deletion (all interior vowels are dropped). The variation is particularly effective in abbreviating short or one-syllable words (Streeter, Ackroff, & Taylor, 1983). It may also be used for longer words, but is usually further shortened by fixed length truncation.

Phonics

Phonics is the only abbreviation method based on sound. It replaces syllables with letters having similar pronunciations. Using phonics, N, XPONT, and XTEND become the representations for END, EXPONENT, and EXTEND. The method produces abbreviations that resemble vowel deletion, and evokes the antecedent word about as well (Hirsh-Pasek, Nudelman, & Schneider, 1982).

Concatenation

Concatenation merges words. It is typically used with other abbreviation techniques, especially truncation. Acronyms are well-known examples of the method. They are formed by taking the first letters of words in a phrase and merging them to form a pseudoword such as laser (light amplifies by stimulated emission of radiation).

Discussion and Summary

The traits desired in an abbreviation scheme are ease of learning, minimal effort to shorten the full name, and the capacity of the mnemonic to readily evoke the antecedent. No abbreviation technique is ideal. Different aspects of programming and different types of names require different abbreviation strategies. For example, learning an abbreviation scheme and using it to create code are the primary considerations in software development. But for maintenance, name comprehension is the trait most valued.

Truncation

The truncation method abbreviates full words by deleting one or more trailing letters of the complete name. Among the basics, it gives the best overall results (Hirsh-Pasek, Nudelman, & Schneider, 1982; Streeter, Ackroff, & Taylor, 1983; Rogers & Moeller, 1984; Benbasat & Wand, 1984). It is particularly well suited for abbreviating multisyllable words (Taft & Forster, 1976; Streeter, Ackroff, & Taylor, 1983). The resultant members are short, and resemble the abbreviations people naturally generate (Hodge & Pennington, 1973). Truncation is often used with other abbreviation methods.

There are notable differences between minimum-to-distinguish and fixed-length truncation methods. The former is easier for abbreviating full words when compared to most techniques (Hirsh-Pasek, Nudelman, & Schneider, 1982). However, it fares poorly in other evaluations. The necessity to have knowledge of all dictionary entries before the method can be confidently used creates a significant problem for the maintainer. As the number of abbreviations increases, the programmer runs the risk of employing the same abbreviation for more than one word. Another problem is that mnemonics shortened to only a letter or two may cause confusion to a programmer unfamiliar with a system or if the abbreviation is used sparingly. How many programmers do you think would know that ST is the abbreviation for STORED DATA? Such abbreviations must be used with caution.

Fixed-length deletion compares much better to the other techniques. It is the superior method for both learning an abbreviation system and generating mnemonics from full words. The technique produces mnemonics that are easy to decipher, performing close to the level achieved by phonics and vowel deletion contraction. One problem with this method is in producing unique abbreviations. As the fixed length decreases, the probability of words abbreviating to the same mnemonic rises. One solution is to allow exceptions to the truncation rule. For example, if EXPONENT and EXPAND were to be abbreviated to three characters, the first one encountered would be truncated to EXP, and the second abbreviated to something like XPA or XPO. This solution, however, introduces another problem. Eventually a point will be reached where another exception will destroy the effectiveness of the rule. Increasing the fixed length will correct the problem. Another solution is a hierarchically structured naming table (Streeter, Ackroff, & Taylor, 1983). In it abbreviations are grouped and defined by context. A mnemonic that is valid in one context could mean nothing in another, and refer to something entirely different in a third. For example, the mnemonic CAL could represent CALIPERS when in a program segment about the garage, be without definition in a garden section, and refer to CALORIE in a routine about cooking.

The drawbacks to fixed-length truncation are few, and can generally be surmounted. Its simplicity and effectiveness in all measures of performance make it a preferred method of abbreviation.

Contraction

Contraction produces the best mnemonics for recalling the antecedent. For that reason, it is highly valued in maintenance.

The method's performance depends on the reader's ability to recognize which letters are missing, insert them into their place, and partition the letters into the syllables of the word to be recalled. With vowel deletion, the consonants alone are assumed to be sufficient for inferring the missing vowels to enable word recall.

One-Syllable Words

For short one-syllable words abbreviated to three letters, vowel deletion seems to work better than truncation (Hirsh-Pasek, Nudelman, & Schneider, 1982; Streeter, Ackroff, & Taylor, 1983). LST more effectively recalls LIST than LIS, and WRT evokes WRITE better than WRI. Vowel deletion has only vowels to select the missing letters from, and their placement is restricted. For LST, a vowel can be inserted into the mnemonic between the first two letters (L_ST), the last two letters (LS_T), interspersed among the consonants (L_S_T), at the end of the abbreviation (LST_), or not at all (LST). Because _ST has a high degree of pairing strength and the lack of saliency for LS, the first partitioning is the most probable consonant structure of the antecedent word. Inserting the set of vowels into the consonant structure produces the candidates LAST, LEST, LIST, LUST, and LYST. The pseudowords LEST and LYST can be easily eliminated. All the remaining words are plausible choices. But given the software context, the maintainer would most likely recall LIST because of its frequent use therein.

A similar process is employed for fixed-length truncation. However, the selection of letters to complete the word is from the entire alphabet, and its placement is either at the end of the mnemonic, or if the word is too short to be abbreviated, no placement at all. Assuming that the program maintainer knows the abbreviation technique used, and is able to quickly differentiate between nonwords and permissible orthographic combinations, the candidates for LIS then are LIS, LISA, LISE, LISH, LISI, LISK, LISO, LISP, LIST, LISU, and LISY. As with vowel deletion, pseudowords (i.e., LIS, LISE, LISO, and LISY) are discarded. This leaves a remaining set that is twice as large as contraction. Using a software context to discriminate among the residual candidates does not identify the intended word either. LISP and LIST are both used by programmers. LIST surfaces as the antecedent word only after a finer-grained analysis is conducted to determine the purpose for which the abbreviation was employed. For short monosyllabic words, vowel deletion produces the better mnemonics.

Multisyllable Words

For multisyllabic words abbreviated to six letters, the opposite holds true. Using vowel deletion, the command SUBSTITUTE abbreviates to SBSTTT. Again the selection of letters used to complete the word is the small set of vowels. But now the consonant structure of the intended word is not as clearly reflected. There are more letters to partition and more syllables to consider. Limiting the reconstruction to the first syllable or two produces a large set of possibilities: SAB*BATH, SAB*O*TAGE, SE*BAS*TIAN, SIB*SHIP, SOB*STUFF, SUB*STAN*TIVE, SUB*STI*TUTE, SYB*A*RITE, and so on. Granted not all programmers are familiar with these words, but they will all initially consider different vowel/consonant structure combinations until the antecedent word is found. The greater the number of combinations to consider, the longer it takes to recognize the intended word. Truncation generates a more effective mnemonic. With six letters, the first one or two syllables are fully displayed. For SUBSTITUTE, the abbreviation is SUBSTI. Considering additional letters may not be necessary. The initial syllables may provide enough information to distinguish it from other considerations. In situations where the antecedent word is long and the mnemonic contains up to six letters, fixed-length truncation is the technique to use.

Summary

There is not one technique that works best for all of the abbreviation tasks and situations found in maintenance. Truncation does the best overall, and is frequently used in combination with other methods. But contraction produces a superior mnemonic for short monosyllabic words, the kind most often encountered in maintenance. Also, phonics and concatenation can be useful in certain situations. Creating effective mnemonics is both art and science. Abbreviation schemes need to take into consideration the vocabularies in use now and in the future.

Chapter 8
Language

Roughly defined, language is a collection of words and the rules governing their association, used to convey and receive thoughts within a community. It is studied to understand how words are, and can be, strung together to inform others.

Proficiency in the use of languages is an integral part of being a programmer. It factors prominently in every phase of software development and maintenance. When programs are well written, they are easy to maintain.

Programmers generally tailor their vocabularies to the needs of their working environments. In the first section, those languages used by programmers are defined and classified. Understanding language acquisition and syntax is the focus of the next section. A mot all software developers should keep in mind is what one programmer writes another must decipher. Finally, a study of computer file names is summarized to assess the state of language usage in programs.

Languages Used by Programmers

Language is the collection of words and symbols used to communicate with others. The dictionary[7] defines it as "the words, their pronunciation, and the methods of combining them used and understood by a considerable community and established by long use." The most familiar language we use is our first language. It is the language we begin to acquire at infancy, and continue to learn throughout adulthood. The word set comprising it is ever changing as new symbols and meanings gain popularity, and others disappear from use. Indigenous languages develop spontaneously in noncontrived environments. They are called the "natural" languages (Cherry, 1986).

Within a natural language, such as English, Japanese, or German, are numerous sublanguages. Some have evolved into "constrained" languages. Others have been deliberately created to form "artificial" languages. Several of each type may be found in one program.

---

[7] *Webster's Third New International Dictionary*, Philip Babcock Cove, Editor, Merriam-Webster, Inc., Springfield, Mass., 1986.

Constrained Languages

A constrained language is a specialized vocabulary of a natural language. It describes phenomena according to the unique perspectives and purposes of a community within the larger population of language users (Pylyshyn, 1984). The language of the group reveals how it interprets the event world.

For example, consider the different ways a computer is seen among an operator, a programmer, and an electrical engineer. Each has a particular interest with respect to the computer, and each employs a specialized vocabulary to express that view. The first is concerned with the operation of either the applied program or the computer itself. An operator's duties may consist of monitoring a computer system's performance, loading and reloading software, or preparing input and output for the computer and user. Reflective of those duties are phrases such as "uptime" and "downtime" (referring to the operation status of the computer), "boot" and "reboot the computer" (meaning to load and reload the basic systems software), and "mount overflow on one" (instructs the operator to hang the overflow tape on drive one). The second's interest is centered on the creation and modification of software. The programmer determines the tasks to be computed, creates software and hardware requirements to accomplish those ends, and generates instructions for the computer to actually perform the tasks. He may use terms such as "decision table" (an array of decisions with their accompanying dispositions), "load under 100K" (the permissible size of the program in the computer), and "source code" (the programmer's coding entries). An engineer is involved with the electronics that enable a program to function. In his world, circuitry is created to execute computer instructions, interface with the end user and computer personnel, and interact with other devices. An electrical engineer uses such words as "AND-gate" (logic circuitry), "CRT" (cathode ray tube), and "bus" (a common electrical channel). Each community has developed a specialized vocabulary that effectively constrains the natural language in ways suited to the tasks and objects confronted.

Constrained languages are of particular concern to the maintenance programmer. Embodied in a program are at least two constrained languages. The programmer uses one that expresses the processing, manipulation, and transfer operations applied to the data. The other is employed by the end user to describe the specific entities and processes to be computed. Thus, if software is written to perform a task in statistics, "mean," "standard deviation," and "t-test" are words originating from the applied domain, and "store," "move," and "retrieve" are terms normally found in the programmer's lexicon. Some terms, such as "add" and "total" belong to both vocabularies.

Artificial Languages

Artificial languages are vocabulary systems typically designed for exact communication within a limited community of users (Perlman, 1984; Cherry, 1986). They are used frequently in research (e.g., MALs), for solving problems (e.g., mathematics), and many other applications.

Programmers both develop and use artificial languages. They create assemblers, compilers, and interpreters to facilitate coding. They also employ them to communicate with the program maintainers (e.g., coding conventions) and end users (e.g., user interfaces).

Language Acquisition and Syntax

A language is a system of semantic and syntactic elements. The semantic part organizes the words and the meanings attached to them. The syntactic portion structures the rules and methods used for combining the words into a more sophisticated form of communication. For an artificial language, it may be thought of as the assignment of roles to the symbols in an expression (Perlman, 1984). Although other views, such as cognitive grammar (see Appendix K) exist, this is the construction most often used.

Language is not acquired until its syntax is learned. One factor influencing the latter's acquisition is semantics (Nagata, 1976). A clear understanding of what the names in a convention represent increases the programmer's ability to determine the rules for combining them.

Syntactic knowledge is transferable. Combinatorial rules learned in one section of a routine can be used to understand another portion of the code. Similar concepts are usually expressed by similar syntactic constructions (Palermo & Parrish, 1971; Perlman, 1984).

The primary hindrances to syntactic acquisition are its modification and complexity. A change in syntax will effect a more noticeable drop in language comprehension than will a substitution of a different name for one that is regularly used (Landauer et al., 1983). An increase in syntactic complexity produces a corresponding increase in the time needed to obtain language proficiency (Chechile, Fleischman, & Sadoski, 1986), and a greater reliance on semantic knowledge for sentence comprehension (Nagata, 1976). Syntax acquisition is also impaired if there are multiple representations for the same function, or if several operations are denoted by the same symbol or word (Reisner, 1981).

In general, people have a tendency to resist learning unfamiliar conventions for naming entities and functions (Reisner, 1977). When faced with the task, they will try to decipher the meaning of new symbols and discover the rules of syntax from the knowledge that they currently possess. Although often correct in their assessments, they may arrive at conclusions that are inappropriate or in error.

Language Usage in Programs

In the course of writing and maintaining software, programmers create artificial languages through the names they give to variables, routines, and files. The names serve as memory aids to the programmers, and as a means for interpreting the code to all future maintainers. A study of program names (Carroll, 1982) shows the usage, structures, and traits of these artificial languages.

Indexed Names

A popular naming structure is the index. The form consists of a stem that is either prefixed or suffixed with a sequential string of alphanumeric characters (e.g., ADATA, BDATA, CDATA, or DATA1, DATA2, DATA3). It is used to order a series of file names, or to group a number of referents under a common name.

Compound Names

Compound names are frequently encountered in a programming environment. They are rule schemes (e.g., NAME____, ____NAME), but do not usually follow a universal plan. Programmers often use them to group a project's files together, and thereby avoid time-consuming searches through directory listings.

Compound names are typically ad hoc inventions with little thought given to existing naming patterns. Programmers often find many names able to claim membership in more than one rule scheme. A small constrained scheme may be contained in a larger pattern, or one pattern may serve as the blueprint for another. Some names reflect an interstructuring of two rule schemes from the same morphology (e.g., CONHEAD, GENHEAD, MUSHEAD, NEWCONF, NEWGEN, and NEWMUS). Such metaschemes are more abstract than single patterns, and the names they refer to tend to be employed for the same application. As new names are added, the rule schemes of existing names become less distinct.

New names should be coextensions of existing rule schemes, but often they are ill formed, conflicting, or form spurious patterns. Anomalous structures arise when the same abbreviation is used for different referents, or if one referent is represented by more than one mnemonic. For example, abbreviations standing for unrelated functions, but containing the same initial letter sequences, suggest a relationship that does not exist. Programmers encountering ALLIST and ALLOCA for the first time would probably have trouble discerning that the former refers to "Al's list" and the latter to "allocate." Ambiguity also occurs when different letter sequences refer to the same operation (e.g., CONSP and SPOOL both denote spooling functions). Although some of the anomalous patterns might be caused by name length restrictions, the primary cause is a lack of awareness of existing patterns and their meanings.

Parts of Speech

The part of speech of a name corresponds to its usage within a program. Procedures and routines have verbs for names. Objects receive names that are nouns.

Whether an object has a simple or compound name depends on the namer's familiarity with the referent. Names that are simple nouns have proceeded further in the shortening process than compound head names. More of the antecedent description has been incorporated into the namer's semantic memory, requiring only a simple cue to bring its intended meaning into consciousness.

Referents with compound head names need multiple cues to effect the same result.

Abbreviation Techniques

Most of the names studied were either not abbreviated or were a concatenation of words. When an abbreviation was used, the preferred technique was truncation. It occurred four times as often as contraction. Frequently the abbreviations contained visual, phonetic, or symbol features of the name description (e.g., D3 for "data-directed dialogue"). In some mnemonics the inferred name elements were reordered to rearrange file listings, reposition the head verb to the last part of the name, or place the more salient element first.

Chapter 9
Language of Mnemonics

A language of mnemonics is a naming convention designed for maintaining software. The names it provides augment the maintainer's ability to solve problems, and enable program refinements and corrections to be made more quickly and more accurately.

In this chapter, the rationale used to develop a language of mnemonics is presented. The initial sections cover the human factors considered in the language's design. First, it is argued that programmers should write software for the maintainers of the code. Those programmers may be entry-level coders or highly skilled experts, and have different information-seeking behaviors and processing needs. The next section discusses memory in relationship to programs, and other factors affecting information processing. Writing a naming convention requires knowledge of the tasks to be performed. In the third section, those tasks are broken down into their component parts.

In the last section, techniques for constructing a language are presented. They give the information specialist or systems designer the means for tailoring information to the anticipated needs of the maintainer.

Writing Code for the Maintainers

Programmers, in a sense, are akin to writers and speakers. Each use language to convey thoughts and ideas. And, each must consider his audience to communicate effectively.

One difficulty in writing code for maintainers is the disparity in skills that exists among programmers. They may be at any skill level within the range of novice to expert. The challenge is to write programs that meet the needs of both extremes, and also serve the maintainer whose talents fall somewhere in between. Each group possesses unique characteristics, and has different information needs.

In the discussion that follows, a novice programmer refers to individuals that have never been exposed to a programming language. Those considered to be an expert have more than one year's experience writing code.

Novice Programmers

The novice programmer lacks the robust cognitive structures that develop from extensive use of computer languages to solve problems. Those associations are just beginning to form. When asked to recall lines of code, the novice will concentrate on the minute details of the program (Black & Sebrechts, 1981). At this stage of development, language is internally structured into syntactic categories (Adelson, 1981), or is paired with prior knowledge that is unrelated to programming (Reisner, 1977; McKeithen et al., 1981). The internal organization of a language varies widely among novices (McKeithen et al., 1981; Adelson, 1981; Landauer et al., 1983).

Generally, novices expect language to be consistent, and make errors when anomalies are encountered (Reisner, 1977). The software designer should be aware of two needs of the beginning programmer. First, information is best conveyed in a natural language form, and should not require additional references in order to be understood (McKeithen et al., 1981). And second, as the novice becomes more skilled, the need for self-explanatory, English-like expressions abates, and eventually is no longer useful (Eason & Damodaran, 1981).

Expert Programmers

Expert programmers possess a highly developed internal structure of associations. They have arranged language into a larger array of perceptual chunks than novices have (Chase & Simon, 1973), and utilize their knowledge of programming to recall software segments (McKeithen et al., 1981). Experts are better able to discern computer code and develop an abstract representation of the program's overall structure (Black & Sebrechts, 1981). Their internal language structure reflects a functional utility in meeting software objectives (McKeithen et al., 1981; Adelson, 1981). Because experts have common problem-solving experiences, their internal structures are similar (McKeithen et al., 1981; Adelson, 1981).

The software designer should cater to the expert's preference for abbreviated information, and consider the naming convention that he has developed (Nickerson, 1969).

Skill Level Comparison

The overall relationship that exists among programmers of different skill levels can be determined by comparing their internal representations of a computer language. The resulting analysis takes the shape of a cone. Spread out at the base of the cone are the novices. As a group, they have the fewest number of memory chunks in common. Intermediate programmers populate the middle section. Their cognitive structures are more similar. At the top of the cone are the programmers who have the most representations in common, the experts. Among the groups, novice and intermediate programmers have more chunks in common with the experts than they have with members of their own skill level (McKeithen et al., 1981).

Organization and Processing

Memory organization and information processing affect the programmer's cognitive state, and hence his effectiveness in maintaining software.

Memory Organization

Information is recalled according to the way it was structured upon entry into memory. How a programmer cues memory (i.e., writing code) affects what the maintainer will later recall. When a memory chunk is accessed, each item in the chunk is recalled before processing on the next chunk begins. This is reflected in software by the location of programming errors. More of them occur at the boundaries of program phrases than within the phrase (Norcio & Kerst, 1983).

The relationship of recall and memory organization becomes more apparent as program complexity increases. For only a few items, a structure is not helpful. However, to identify a large number of referents, an elaborate organization may be required. The degree to which information is structured varies directly with the amount of information with which the programmer has to contend (Buschke, 1976). People organize information according to what they feel is needed for future recall (Scapin, 1981).

Information Processing

The information processing capabilities and needs of the programmer affect how well software will be developed and maintained. One factor, short-term memory, has a direct bearing on development. Programmers with a large STM capacity make fewer errors when writing code than those whose memory is small (Norcio & Kerst, 1981). Also affecting a programmer's performance is the amount of information to be communicated, the rate of information flow, and the capacity of the maintainer to assimilate information. Each of these can be controlled through the software's naming convention and coding structure.

Another problem is the availability of information. Useful and much needed information will not be used if it is not accessible and convenient to the programmer (Norman & Bobrow, 1975; Chechile, Fleischman, & Sadoski, 1986). The point is illustrated in documentation. Extensive documentation accompanying software is usually not read (James, 1981). The software designer has a better chance to communicate through the program's names and comments. Information in that form is at hand, and much of the need for external references is eliminated.

Maintenance Tasks

Maintenance programmers are expected to be proficient in correcting errant software and enhancing a program's capabilities.

To correct a program deficiency, a programmer might do the following.

1. Analyze the anomaly.
2. Locate the error in the program.
3. Correct the error.
4. Test for errors. If no errors are found, the goal is achieved. If errors persist, repeat the sequence starting at the first step.

For enhancing a program the maintainer could do the following.

1. Analyze the modification to be made.
2. Locate the program segment(s) to be modified.
3. Incorporate the modification into the software.
4. Test and debug. If error free, the goal is attained. If errors are present, employ the correct software procedure.

Although each plan is designed to achieve a different goal, the detailed procedures are alike in many respects. Common to both plans are the steps to locate code segments and to test for errors. Actually, the test and debug procedure of the program enhancement plan is, for the most part, the plan for correcting program deficiencies.

Names can be used to increase the programmer's efficiency in locating code segments and testing. The former procedure can be further broken down into a comprehension component, in which the variables, routines, and files are assessed according to their utility in achieving the goal of the plan, and a code-finding subtask that guides the programmer through the software to either the error or the code segment to be modified. Appropriately chosen names will assist the maintainer in discerning the code and understanding how it relates to the program. They also can reflect the location in the program where the referent has been assigned a value, and therefore eliminate a time-consuming search to uncover an error. It is with these uses of a name that the language of mnemonics is primarily concerned.

Language of Mnemonics

Computer code is the interface between the internal workings of the machine and the mind. It is created from a computer language, such as a compiler. Using it, the programmer assigns names that are meaningful to some future maintainer.

The Target Audience

The initial activity in creating a naming convention is to decide what is the target audience, what messages need to be conveyed, and what language to use to communicate them.

The novice programmer requires considerably more information than the seasoned professional. When the number of messages is large, a natural language is the appropriate medium to use (Rich, 1984). Experts, however, are able to generate and maintain programs written in constrained artificial languages, and do them more quickly and with fewer errors (Curtis, 1981; Miller, 1981; Perlman, 1984).

Although it is tempting to write code for novices, priority should be given to the needs of experts. Novices are in a state of transition. Soon they will become more proficient at programming, and their information needs will be more like the experts'. Code should satisfy the experts' preference for mnemonics. The information needs of novices can be met by using the comments feature of programming languages as a gloss.

Naming

Constrained languages make effective naming conventions. Problems can be solved as well with them as with unrestricted vocabularies (Kelly & Chapanis, 1977).

Crucial to the effectiveness of a mnemonic interface are the pairings of names to concepts (Rich, 1984). Names should never be casually assigned. For optimal utility, names should be assigned only after an information specialist has decided which concepts will be utilized in the program, and only after those concepts have been separated into distinct referents and formally defined. Until this has been done, any attempt at naming will increase the likelihood that the names given will be ill-structured and ambiguous. Astutely structuring mental images and concepts through the selection of meaningful names increases the maintainer's productivity because the representation of the event world is made more distinct and discernible (Perlman, 1984; Chaudary & Sahasrabuddhe, 1985).

After the referents have been named, they need to be systematically abbreviated. The method used (e.g., Ehrenreich, 1985) should be selected on its ability to ensure that the first syllable of the antecedent word or phrase is easily recognized. The more popular abbreviation lengths are three and four characters (Benbasat, Dexter, & Masulis, 1981; Gabriele & Frauenhofer, 1984). However, mnemonics containing a single letter are not uncommon (Gabriele & Frauenhofer, 1984).

The language of mnemonics (e.g., Smith, 1981) employs three structures to convey information: indices, bigrams, and descriptive matrixes.

Table 3. Mnemonic Creation.

The Shortening Process		
Full Description	Name	Mnemonic
The <u>format</u> displaying data values from calculations based on direct <u>measurements</u>.	<u>Mea</u>surement <u>Format</u>	MEAFMT
The <u>flag</u> that determines when the <u>format</u> is used.	<u>Format</u> <u>Flag</u>	FMTFLG
<u>Calculate</u> the standard <u>deviation</u>.	<u>Cal</u>culate <u>Dev</u>iation	CALDEV
<u>Generate</u> all <u>calculations</u> requested by the end user.	<u>Gen</u>erate <u>Cal</u>culations	GENCAL

Indices

Indices consist of four-character mnemonic stems appended by two-digit sequential numbers. They are used to represent large families of referents, such as a series of arrays (ARRY01,... , ARRY99) or sort routines (SORT01,... , SORT99), and artifacts whose functions are well known and to whose identification additional information would not significantly contribute. By using index structures, irrelevant items can be disposed of quickly, freeing up cognitive resources for other pertinent tasks. For example, software may contain a number of diagnostic routines that dump the contents of variables in a variety of formats. They are used to track down errors and to ensure that a modification has been made correctly. Because there may be a number of dump routines, and because they are not part of the primary function of the program, they are ideal candidates for representation by an index format. A programmer scanning the program can readily discern its function, dismiss it, and continue on to the desired segment of code. The mnemonic stem may assume any part of speech.

Bigrams

Bigrams (Carroll, 1981, 1983; Rosenberg, 1983) are composed of two agglutinated three-character mnemonic units (i.e., AAABBB, where AAA and BBB are three-character mnemonic units), and are used where fuller descriptions of referents are needed.

Using two mnemonics enables the information specialist to describe referents in phrases and sentences. Noun and adjective constructions can uniquely represent most variables and files, and organize referents into groups. For example, ERR can be used in a general name, such as ERRCOD (error code), to denote a group, and in more specific names that describe its members: FMTERR (format error), ZDVERR (zero divide error), and THRERR (threshold error). Routines and procedure files may use a sentence format to represent the action nature of their contents. Thus, if the information specialist were asked to provide names for a series of statistic routines to calculate the mode, median, and standard deviation, he might name them CALMOD, CALMED, and CALSTD.

Descriptor Matrices

Descriptor matrices create distinct names for groups of related referents sharing common nameheads. Their abstract form is similar to bigrams. Each namehead is represented by a three-character mnemonic that appears in the first mnemonic-word position. The second position is replaced with three, single-character descriptor positions. The additional information provided by the descriptors serves to distinguish the items having a common namehead. The descriptors are organized into groups, which are in turn structured into a matrix.

Table 4. Descriptor Matrix.

Character Position		
1st	2nd	3rd
C—calculated value	A—value at reference point A	A—atmospheric pressure
M—measure value	B—value at reference point B	L—lower heating value
N—no value or neutral value	M—mean of values at reference points A and B	B—correcting for both conditions
	N—no value or neutral value	N—no value or neutral value

The structure can be used to keep track of the transformations that are applied to a set of input variables as they progress through a program. To illustrate, consider the variables describing an airplane engine's fuel flow (EFF). At the start of the program, engine fuel flow has no descriptors (N) associated with it (EFFNNN). Once the program has evaluated the set of constraints under which it will operate, the mnemonic stem will need to be described in greater detail. If EFF represents a value measured directly (M), as opposed to one that has been calculated from other variables, it is noted in the name (EFFMNN). The end user may want to know the rate of fuel flow at different points within the engine. A reading requested at point A (A) is therefore reflected in the name (EFFMAN). Fuel flow may be corrected for atmospheric pressure (A), a lower heating value (L), or be adjusted for both conditions (B). If both calculations are performed, the variable is named EFFMAB. In this way the designer is able to provide unique names at each step in the transformation process.

Using a single-letter mnemonic has a serious drawback. A letter designated to represent one item may also represent another referent within the given context. To be effective, a mnemonic needs to both cue the desired name and inhibit the activation of other representations. Thus, trouble could arise in the preceding illustration if the mean average of fuel flows at engine reference points A and B is requested. Usually, such problems can be resolved by carefully selecting the words to be abbreviated. In the case described, using the word mean (M) to denote the concept will eliminate the conflict of using A for both mean average and point A. In other situations, the designer may not be so fortunate, and may need to use numbers as descriptors. The numbers will not initially cue the sought-after names, but they will not cause any misconceptions to be formed either. Through use, the numbers will become associated with the referents (Perlman, 1984).

The Language in Operation

Taken together, the three structures give the designer the capability to sculpture knowledge to fit the needs of the maintenance programmer. The indices enable the programmer to quickly discern a variable's general function, discard it, and continue on to a desired program segment. For more elaborate descriptions, the bigram format is used. The additional information may point to where the referent entered the program, or simply distinguish it from related functions. Bigrams, if they are astutely constructed, will reflect the task environment and assist the programmer in maintaining software. If the source of the variable's value can be discerned from the name, time-consuming searches through software can be eliminated when troubleshooting. Through descriptor matrices, a large number of referents can be uniquely defined. They also provide a structure for creating new names. Descriptors tell the maintainer which processing steps have been performed. They form coding trails through which variables can be traced to the place where they take on values.

Summary

Affecting maintenance are the names given to variables, routines, and files. They represent referents, their function within a program, and attributes that facilitate the completion of maintenance tasks. For some referents, it is desirable to use general terms. They will enable the maintainer to quickly discern their functions, and dismiss them if they are not relevant to the present task. For others, more detail is needed. By structuring names, cognitive resources can be more effectively deployed. Good representations reflect the task environment of the expert maintainer, and are abbreviated with a scheme that preserves the first syllable of the antecedent word. Information can be tailored for the maintainer through indices, bigrams, and descriptive matrices.

Section III
Solutions Through Structure

Chapter 10
More on Problem Solving

Chapters 10 through 13 make up a section on the program's structure. The structure of a program may either facilitate or hinder maintenance. It regulates the flow of information, and in conjunction with referent names, aids cognition. An effective structure assembles the symbols of a program into forms that enhance problem solving.

Section Overview

This, the first chapter of the section, discusses information processing and its role in problem solving, and describes how novices and experts solve problems. In the next chapter, "Solving Maintenance Problems," the methods that a maintainer employs to modify and correct code are examined. Coding errors and obstructions, expert and novice skill differences, and cognitive processing limitations are covered in Chapter 12 ("Other Considerations"). In the section's concluding chapter, "Cognitive Structures," a software organization to improve the performance of maintenance tasks is presented.

Utilizing Information

The tasks that a maintainer performs are accomplished by utilizing information. Some parts of the job may be routine, and require only that a procedure be recalled from memory and employed. For example, using a computer language or searching for a section of code have typically been done many times, and the activity needs merely to be recognized as a goal before a body of information is retrieved to do it. When such plans and procedures do not exist, the maintainer is faced with a problem.

To solve a problem, one must fully comprehend the situation causing concern, and then assemble a new set of relationships to accomplish the goal. This is how information is used within the gestalt school of psychology (see Appendix L).

Solving Problems with Gestalt Psychology

Gestalt psychology is the study of conceptual wholes. Problems are defined as incomplete concepts, and are resolved when a new configuration of information makes the thought whole. The new configurations of the problem state are called "insights." They occur once the problem situation is thoroughly understood, and signify that a new set of relationships is seen that better fits the solution criteria. That is, it is understood how the features contained in the problem's elemental parts can be realigned to more completely achieve the goal (Kanizsa, 1979). The understanding is intuitive when the restructuring is rapid, and the problem solver is unaware of the processes that generated the perception (Simon, 1986). Usually accompanying an insight is the "aha" experience. It indicates that the new configuration is clearly perceived for the first time, as though "a veil has been lifted from my eyes" (Kanizsa, 1979). A period of incubation is required before it can occur (Simon, 1986).

There will be many partial insights to a number of subproblems en route to an overall solution to a complex problem. Each partial insight reveals new relationships that contribute to the way the problem is understood, and thereby leads to its solution (Kanizsa, 1979). How fast the problem is solved is determined by the rate at which they occur (Simon, 1986).

Problems that are well structured and described are much easier to solve than ones that are not. A representation is considered well posed if it meets these conditions:

1. The representation is isomorphic to the problem's actual structure.
2. In the representation, all of the problem's components are interrelated.
3. The representation is consistent with other knowledge possessed by the problem solver.

Well-defined representations facilitate problem solving because the elemental components of the problem are easy to reconfigure, and the way to meet the criteria for a solution is apparent (Wertheimer cited in Simon, 1986). This happens when words access a robust set of relationships among the problem's basic components, and the problem solver is able to think of a variety of transformations to apply to it (Kanizsa, 1979; Simon, 1986; Woods & Roth, 1988).

Means-End Analysis

An illustration of how information is manipulated to solve problems is means-end analysis (Newell & Simon, 1972; Winston, 1977; Nilsson, 1980). It posits a problem space that contains all the states the problem can assume, any transformation operation that can be applied to them, and any description needed in processing. The problem's initial and goal states are also defined. Solutions to the problem are proposed in the form of plans made up of sets of procedures, and are applied to either the initial or goal state. When procedures are found that concretely connect the goal and initial states, the problem is solved. Otherwise, new plans are constructed, and the process is repeated (Polya cited in Shneiderman, 1980).

Problem-Solving Factors

Obtaining a solution to a problem is not always as easy and as straightforward as the preceding discussion suggests. Some problems by their nature are more difficult than others, and require a goodly amount of effort to resolve. How much effort is determined by the amount of knowledge needed to effect a solution, the demands placed on memory, the representation of the problem, and under certain conditions problem size. All of the factors are interrelated.

The amount of information and knowledge required to solve a problem, including the problem's representation, is a quantitative measure that varies in direct proportion to its difficulty. The more objects and processes there are to define and relate, the more difficult the problem becomes (Kotovsky & Simon, 1990).

Problem difficulty is determined mostly, however, by the quality of the problem representation, and the degree to which it facilitates understanding (Kotovsky & Simon, 1990). Its effectiveness is determined, in part, by our capacity to receive the information presented. Problems that are framed in domains that we understand well can be described with fewer symbols, and are solved more readily than those that are not (Matson & Johnson-Laird cited in Kotovsky & Simon, 1990). Another factor is the stability of the representation. It affects the amount of problem information that can be stored in working memory. Structures that are undergoing change require more space than stable units (Kotovsky, Hayes, & Simon, 1985). Also affecting processing is the degree to which an item can be described. One referent having several attributes can be kept track of more easily than several entities described by a solitary trait (Kotovsky, Hayes, & Simon, 1985). These characteristics make programs more maintainable, and manifest themselves as stable mnemonic languages and structures that facilitate change, and as pertinent documentation.

The demand for memory is one more factor determining problem-solving difficulty. To solve problems quickly, a small area in memory is needed for planning. Complex problems take longer to solve because the type or amount of information they generate places large demands on limited resources. If the problem solver is burdened with learning the elementary rules of a new domain, or if the rules are complex, working memory may soon become overloaded (Kotovsky, Hayes, & Simon, 1985; Kotovsky & Simon, 1990). Simplifying the process makes available more resources for planning, and reduces the time to solve problems. Therefore, if programs can be expressed using a few elementary rules that may be combined in a number of different ways in lieu of specialized instruction sequences, they will be more effectively maintained.

Problem size refers to the size of the decision tree used to represent a problem space. It is a predictor of problem-solving difficulty only when the decisions of which path to follow are made in a random, trial-and-error manner (Kotovsky, Hayes, & Simon, 1985). Problem spaces, however, are rarely searched that way. The determinant for the most part can be discounted (Kotovsky & Simon, 1990).

Problem-Solving Behavior

Solving problems is an iterative process. Many solutions will be proposed and rejected before a candidate meeting the solution criteria is found. It is through the failures that success is achieved. Analyzing the rejected proposals is how we learn more about the problem. Each new insight transforms the problem space, bringing us incrementally closer to a solution. Problem solving is the continual restructuring of problem components until a solution is reached. And, the ability to reconfigure information is a common trait among problem solvers (Kanizsa, 1979).

Experts and novices solve problems differently. To facilitate maintenance, programs will need to accommodate the expert without hindering the novice.

The Expert

The expert is able to function at a high level of proficiency because he has a rich collection of knowledge and information about the problem domain, and knows how to work effectively within it. He solves the problem from an understanding of the principles governing the attributes of the problem's elements (Kanizsa, 1979). He has the ability to capture and process the salient aspects of the problem, and utilize information to effect change within the event world of the problem space. He knows the permissible transformation operations that can be applied to a particular state, and the resulting state the operation will produce. The expert solves the problem by working immediately towards the solution from the initial problem state. The problem is quickly assessed, new elements inserted where needed, and a plan is loosely constructed to achieve a solution. Plans will contain one or more unknowns to be solved. Solving these will lead to other unknowns, which will also be solved. A solution is realized when a path emerges from the initial state to a goal state that is free of unknowns (Kanizsa, 1979).

The Novice

The novice is not as fortunate. He lacks the rich body of knowledge and information about the problem domain possessed by the expert, and has little choice but to use a general problem-solving procedure such as means-end analysis. With him, solving problems begins at a solution state, and proceeds to the problem situation. The process of defining the goal through a plan in terms of meeting subgoals, subgoals by subplans, proceeds as before, and ends when all of the subgoals can be expressed from known primitives. The novice then works forward to establish a path from the problem situation to the solution state.

Besides a paucity of domain knowledge, the novice is additionally hampered by needing a larger area in limited storage memory for goal accounting. This leaves little room for the detailed planning a novice requires to work both backwards and forwards. The expert, because of his rich knowledge base, is able to use a nonspecific shallow plan that proceeds forward immediately towards a solution.

Summary

The tasks that a maintainer performs are accomplished by utilizing information. Some parts of the job are routine, and require only that a procedure be recalled from memory and employed. When such plans and procedures do not exist, the maintainer is faced with a problem.

Gestalt psychology is the study of conceptual wholes. Problems are defined as incomplete concepts, and are resolved when a new configuration of information makes the thought whole.

Problems that are well structured and described are much easier to solve than ones that are not.

Some problems require a goodly amount of effort to solve. How much effort is determined by the amount of knowledge needed to effect a solution, the demands placed on memory, the representation of the problem, and under certain conditions problem size.

The expert and the novice solve problems differently. The expert possesses a rich description of the problem domain, and uses a nonspecific shallow plan to proceed forward immediately towards a solution. The novice is not blessed with this in-depth understanding. His plans are more detailed, and are directed first backwards to attain goals and subgoals, and then forwards to establish a path from the problem situation to a solution state.

Chapter 11
Solving Maintenance Problems

Solving the problems that arise in software is the primary task of the maintainer. The problem definition, including the solution criteria and any additional information that is needed, is contained in a modification request or an error report. Transformation operations (e.g., adding, deleting, replacing, or rearranging code) are applied as required to the problem situation (i.e., the current state of the code) until the solution criteria are satisfied, ensuring that the other program functions operate as before. Throughout the process, the maintainer relies on timely and appropriate information.

Solving maintenance problems is accomplished by processing and utilizing information. In the chapter's first section, Understanding the Maintenance Request, the focus is on ways to clarify the goals to be achieved in the maintenance task. Program Comprehension follows, and describes how maintainers process program information and how information is acquired. The last section, Modifying the Code, proffers a criterion for a successful alteration of the program.

Understanding the Maintenance Request

The maintenance request describes the changes proposed for the program. In terms of problem solving, it defines the goal(s). To fully understand it, the maintainer needs to be familiar with the program's specifications and requirements, including any modifications made, and the vocabularies used therein.

Basically, a program is the end product of a series of mappings from the event world to expressions of operators and operands, using a programming language. In the course of its construction, a number of knowledge domains will have been employed. The problem, computer language, new knowledge, algorithm, and translation are some of the domains frequently used (Brooks, 1981). Although each is a somewhat different language, fine-grained distinctions are not typically made. Only those that contribute to program comprehension, such as the applied and computer domains, need to be preserved. The others can be subsumed under these dialects. Understanding the maintenance request is, in part, understanding the adjustments to the original mapping.

The maintenance request is understood by programmers to the degree it can be related to the language and structure of the program. Understanding is improved if the request is written in terms associated with software constructions, and the maintainer is included in the process. It is also enhanced if the programmer can quickly see how to alter the code. Therefore, software needs to be structured to accommodate change, and to depict its functions lucidly. Ensuring that the specifications and support documentation describe the software in use is another way to increase understanding.

Understanding the maintenance request is an important first step in resolving a problem. It provides direction for all subsequent activity.

Program Comprehension

To make the requested software changes, the program must be understood. The maintainer needs to identify the coding segment to be altered, determine its characterizing features, and become aware of the relationships it forms with other constructions, whether in the same context or in other domains. Extracting such information is difficult. Software becomes harder to understand as it is maintained. Code designed to be lucid and discernible, having a hierarchical structure (Brooks, 1976), will deteriorate and its conventions will be violated.

Processing the Code

Large programs are complex, and must be processed into abstract forms that can be readily used by the programmer. If the maintainer tried to understand software directly from the instruction sequence, he would be overwhelmed with information. Abstract forms reduce the program to its essential features and component structures, and combine with other information possessed by the programmer (e.g., the program language, algorithms, etc.), to cognitively build an equivalent software mechanism. Through them a programmer is able to modify and correct software.

The programmer uses four types of abstract information: the goals of a program, the flow of data, the flow of control, and conditionalized actions (Pennington, 1987).

Goals

Goal abstractions represent summaries of program segments and their relationships to other components. They are depicted as a hierarchy of associations. At the top of the tree is the overall goal of the program. Each succeeding tier below it contains the subgoals used to accomplish the goal(s) at the immediate higher level. Lines of code are at the leaf nodes. The actual procedures used to attain the goals are not kept. They can be functionally recreated using the goal and other information available to the programmer.

Programmers utilize abstract goal information to locate and modify sections of code. The hierarchical structure provides a rough map of the program that is critical for maintaining software. It orients the maintainer within the instruction sequence, allowing him to navigate from the section of code he is presently viewing to the segment to be altered. The relational information may also be used to ensure that the modified instructions do not affect other program functions.

Data Flow

In a typical program, data enter from an input device, go through a series of processes, and are transferred back into the event world. Data flow abstract forms are the information that has been retained about these events. They are created as the constants and variables of the program are read, and become the data flow of the program when the causal relationships among the referents are assembled.

Data-flow abstractions can be used to infer the general goal structure, and when combined with other information, enable a more detailed construction of the goal hierarchy. They help the programmer determine the ordinal relationships among variables (i.e., variables used in the creation of other variables), and locate the place where a modification is to occur or an errant variable has been assigned an anomalous value.

Control Flow

Control-flow abstract forms represent the execution order of program events (i.e., functional units of processing made up of one or more lines of code). They are most relevant in complex programs where the processing order may be interrupted either by subroutines or by directing the execution to another part of the program. In simple programs, events are processed in a linear sequence and are not problematic.

Control-flow abstractions are used more for understanding event processing within a section of code than for comprehending the program as a whole or for locating a particular segment. These latter tasks are typically achieved with goal structure and data-flow information. The former is employed to modify code or to correct an error caused by the order in which events are processed.

Control-flow information bears a structural resemblance to data-flow abstract forms. It may be used to derive the program's data-flow and goal hierarchy, although the information it provides may not be complete or readily apparent.

Conditionalized Actions

The fourth abstraction type depicts the program's response to different sets of conditions. It may be thought of as a decision table in which every condition is paired to a consequence, or as a production system composed of a series of condition-action statements. In the latter, actions are generated whenever the condition portion of the statement is satisfied. When processed they bring into existence new conditions. The new conditions in turn will meet the condition requirements of other statements, and cause more actions to fire. The cycle continues until a terminating action is processed.

Conditionalized action abstract forms are used to locate and understand sections of code. They have different characteristics than the other types discussed. Extracting goal, data-flow, and control-flow information from them is difficult, and the other abstraction types do not easily produce conditionalized action statements.

Acquiring Program Knowledge

To utilize information, the maintainer has to acquire event world data about the program, and process them into abstract forms. Helping to determine what is acquired and processed are the context of the data and the cognitive state of the programmer.

An understanding of a program means that an accurate model of it has been internally created. The representation will not be complete. It will be tailored to fit only the immediate purposes of the maintainer. The process is similar to name creation. Both are affected by the degree of involvement in the task, and the need to minimally represent event world data. The features that are acquired from the software are determined by the programmer's goal structure, the context created by the maintenance assignment, and the information network used to process the data.

Context

The context of the problem is set by the maintenance assignment. Most of it is defined by the section of code to be changed. The maintainer is most actively engaged in that portion of the program, and knows it better than any other segment. Although all aspects of the program should be known before modifying it, program size, time constraints, and a passive interest limit the maintainer to only a partial understanding.

The goals pursued to modify programs also help determine the program's context. The tasks used to attain goals require that the program be understood in a different sense. For example, to locate a program segment, software must be understood globally. That is, the maintainer has to know the program's structure, and the causal relationships that exist among its separate components. To alter code, a more detailed understanding of how the instruction sequence works to perform the algorithm is needed. In testing, both global and procedural knowledge are used to ensure that the altered code operates as required, and that other program functions are not disturbed.

Context is defined by both the portions of the program accessed by the maintainer and the types of information used.

Information-Seeking Strategy

Seeking the information necessary to maintain software is difficult in large, complex programs. The process may consume a substantial amount of time and resources, and the understanding achieved is often imperfect.

Knowledge about a program's structure and operation is obtained gradually by refining a succession of hypotheses that have been generated to represent the program. Each hypothesis proposed is tested against the instruction sequence for accuracy (Gould, 1975; Brooks, 1981). The process is both progressive and iterative. Many primary and subsidiary hypotheses will be generated before a veridical account of the program is found (Brooks, 1981). Hypotheses are created from information garnered from the program, the maintainer's knowledge of programming, and other sources. Typically, the first set of hypotheses validated represents the general constructions of the program. These model its overall structure and processing order, its inputs, and its outputs. Subsidiary hypotheses are formed later, and complement the ones initially adopted. They are progressively developed in a top-down, depth-first manner until they can be verified in either the code or in the external documentation. Hypothesis generation enables the programmer to quickly attain an understanding of the program. And, the abstract forms they produce minimize the cognitive space needed to internally represent the maintenance context.

The construction of a program affects its comprehension. As the maintainer builds and refines hypotheses, program elements are related and become interpreted as conceptual wholes. Predicting these wholes is a set of reference points called beacons. Beacons indicate the presence of a structure or procedure, and cue the concept within the mind of the programmer. They are used by the maintainer to verify hypotheses. A referent may have several beacons predicting it. And, the same code features may act as a beacon for more than one concept. Beacons predict referents with varying degrees of certainty (Miller, 1974; Brooks, 1976, 1981).

Information Seeking Tactics

A maintainer uses different techniques to extract information from a program. Pertinent factors of the maintenance task and circumstances are weighed to select an extraction method that seems promising. For example, a maintainer may employ tactics to acquire information regarding the location of an error (Arthur, 1988).

1. *Top-Down.* This method is used at the beginning of the search, when there are no clues to indicate where the error might be. Before it can be used, however, the maintainer must have acquired knowledge of the program's structure and the general functions of the code. If the program can also be visualized, the anomaly will be easier to locate. In pursuing the errant code, all suspicious variables are noted, and are verified by analyzing their flow within the program.

2. *Bottom-Up.* It is used when there is an indication of the error's cause or location. The method operates as its name implies. A variable that is found to have an incorrect value is traced up through the program to the error's source.

3. *Fan-Out.* If the preceding method fails, fan-out is tried. It is similar to bottom-up in that they both start by working backwards from the location of the errant variable. The search through the program using the bottom-up technique is causal. When the fan-out method is employed,

each line of code that has assigned a value to the errant variable is examined.

4. *Fan-In.* Fan-in is used when the other tactics have failed. The maintainer begins at the boundaries of the system or program (i.e., the data entry and exit points), and investigates inward, following the data's flow to the error's source.

Modifying the Code

Modifications are successful only if the other software functions remain unaffected. Added capabilities must work in harmony with existing procedures, and functions that are removed or changed must be handled carefully to ensure that other operations are not disturbed.

The ease or difficulty of the modification assignment is determined by the program's construction. Programs whose functions are well defined and segregated lend themselves to change. They can be readily broken down into component operations, making it easier to see how the modification might be achieved.

Summary

A program is a mapping of a set of user specifications onto a computer language. New requirements and errors make it necessary to update this mapping. An alteration is implemented by understanding the change made to the specification, knowing the current mapping (i.e., the program), and then modifying the code to reflect the change.

The maintenance request states the change or programming goal to be achieved. It should give the maintainer a clear unambiguous description of the maintenance assignment.

Maintainers rely on four types of abstract information to understand the program. Two of them, understanding the program's goal structure and data flow, describe software globally. They enable the maintainer to locate sections of code. The other two, control flow and conditional understanding, are employed to alter the instruction sequence.

The goal structure (i.e., the maintenance request) and the context in which it is applied (i.e., the program) largely determine which information will be captured from software. The information is obtained by forming hypotheses about the program's structure and operation, and then testing them for accuracy by comparing them to the code.

Programs that are readily broken down into functional components are easier to maintain.

Chapter 12
Other Considerations

In programming, there is more to consider than solving user problems. Whether in design, code construction, or maintenance, the programmer should be considerate of the maintainer's nature and working habits. With computer processing costs steadily declining and that of programming increasing, making the maintainer efficient is where the greatest savings can be realized.

The effectiveness of the maintainer can be enhanced in several ways. One is to eliminate or lessen the impact of programming obstacles. Obstructions, such as programming errors and structural barriers, act to inhibit the location and discernment of code segments. Another is to write code that is easily maintained by either a novice or expert programmer. Knowing their memory content, organization, and processing differences provides a basis for constructing more accommodating programs. The third is to be mindful of memory capacity limitations. An awareness of the effects that irrelevant information and processing loads have on memory helps to produce easily read code.

Errors and Barriers

Errors and barriers are nettlesome obstructions that consume resources that might otherwise be spent on software improvements or put to some other use. Each affects software differently. Errors make software less reliable, and produce problems that may be very costly to the organization. Structural barriers impede the completion of maintenance tasks, and shorten the program's useful life.

Errors

An error may be introduced into a program from any of its development or maintenance stages. Most of the problems that arise (up to 80%) can be traced to an errant requirement or design decision (Arthur cited in Arthur, 1988). From whatever the source, errors in programs are normally sorted into syntactic and semantic categories.

Syntactic Errors

Syntactic errors are violations of the computer language rules for writing instructions. They are distributed across instruction categories as follows (Arthur, 1988).

Logic	25%
Module interface	16%
Computation	15%
Input and output	15%
Assignment	14%
Data base	10%
Other	5%

Semantic Errors

Semantic errors originate from misunderstandings programmers have of the event world. They typically arise when internal representations are utilized out of context and are experienced, for example, when a different output is produced than what was expected. They are probably caused by a misinterpretation of a line of code or the failure to recognize an errant instruction and occur when the problem solution becomes incorrectly represented in the programmer's semantic memory. As a result, data values may be out of range or unsorted files merged (Shneiderman, 1980).

Errors are difficult to find and correct because: the programmer must maintain a dynamic model of the program in limited storage memory that keeps track of a number of aspects about the software; programs contain a variety of structures; and programming requires accuracy and a high degree of precision (Gould, 1975).

Correcting Errors

Debugging software does not require a special skill. All that is needed are the abilities to understand programs, locate code segments, and solve problems. Generally, a maintainer who is accomplished in the other phases of programming is also adept at debugging (Gould, 1975).

The time spent finding and correcting errors varies according to error type and context. For example, assignment errors take much longer to correct than iteration and array subscript bugs, because a more thorough understanding of the program is required (Gould & Drongowski, 1974; Gould, 1975; Atwood & Ramsey cited in Sheil, 1981). It is also easier to correct a number of errors in a single program than in a succession of programs, and a series of bugs of the same type are corrected more readily than a varied collection (Gould, 1975).

To correct errors, the maintainer uses information from the program and its output. Clues to the error's location are obtained from the names given to variables, routines, and files. An error is detected because it is inconsistent with nearby constructions. A line of code appears suspicious if there is incongruity among variable names, constants, and operation order; or if the step does not make sense within the instruction sequence. Comments provide additional information. Their value depends on the bug's nature and the construction of the program.

The inputs to the program and interactive debugging systems are not widely used by the maintainer for correcting errors (Gould, 1975).

The maintainer uses cognitive processes similar to those employed for understanding programs when debugging software. Knowledge and information about the anomaly are acquired, processed into hypotheses regarding the location and nature of the bug, and tested against the program for accuracy. If the error is not found, the cycle is repeated (Gould, 1975). The particular debugging strategy chosen by the programmer is influenced by his familiarity with the code, his motivation, the degree of urgency, and the information available. Maintainers tend to eliminate the easier compiler or syntax errors first, and then concentrate on the more demanding semantic bugs (Gould & Drongowski, 1974).

Barriers

The term barrier refers to constructions that interfere with a programmer's ability to readily understand software, locate code segments, and solve problems. For example, a barrier may be the computer language in use that causes certain errors to be committed more frequently than other language (Youngs, 1974). The barriers most troublesome are those created by a poorly designed program or haphazardly performed maintenance task, such as spaghetti code (i.e., undisciplined control flow), unstructured software, functions that are intertwined, multiple programming styles, and ill-chosen names for variables, routines, and files.

Cognitive Processes and Programming

Five cognitive processes determine a maintainer's ability to surmount program barriers (Irons, 1981).

1. *Flexibility closure.* This process is used extensively. It enables the programmer to retain a specific percept in memory, and recognize it in distracting material. During software development, concepts that have been defined in the specifications become incorporated into the design, and from it into the code. Maintainers need to be able to recognize the same percept in each stage.
2. *Associative memory.* It forms relationships among objects and actions, and is used in all programming tasks.
3. *Induction.* The reasoning process, in which general beliefs about a class are adopted once they have been observed in a subset of it, is called induction. It enables concepts to be represented abstractly, and eliminates the need for duplicate information. Induction is a skill used for both

software composition and debugging tasks. It is employed to construct and test hypotheses, and to generate code fragments.

4. *Syllogistic reasoning.* This is a form of deductive reasoning whereby the acceptance of the major and minor premises proves the conclusion (e.g., if A is contained in B, and B is contained in C, then A is contained in C). It is used more in program development than in debugging. Errors associated with read format constructions are linked to faulty syllogistic reasoning.

5. *Spatial scanning.* It is the cognitive process that enables a programmer to quickly peruse a program listing and discover a set of causal relationships running through it. Spatial scanning proficiency is very important when debugging software, and predicts errors in arithmetic expressions and statement construction.

More Novice/Expert Differences

The programmers who maintain software vary widely in ability. Anyone from a novice to an expert may be assigned a maintenance task, and it is not unusual to find that both a novice and an expert have worked on the same code. This creates a problem for structuring software because each expertise level has different information needs. To effectively maintain programs, the information requirements of each must be fully understood and met.

The programmer's semantic and syntactic memories and tactical skill predict maintenance performance (Bateson, Alexander, & Murphy, 1987). The difference between the novice and expert is in the contents, organization, and processing of their memories, and how the expert applies his skills.

Memory Contents

The information possessed by an expert differs from that of a novice in both quantity and quality. The expert is able to draw upon large organized bodies of knowledge that are structured for efficient recall (Vessey, 1987; Bateson, Alexander, & Murphy, 1987). Over the course of his career, he has worked on many programs and has solved many different types of problems. From these experiences, a rich store of knowledge has been built up that can be readily applied to the tasks routinely encountered. The expert relies on this knowledge to acquire a representation of the program's general structure and code functions. The information within the novice's memory is not as developed. He has a tendency to focus on coding details, and creates complex mental representations that are difficult to access (Black & Sebrechts, 1981). This is also true of an expert working on nonroutine tasks (Black & Sebrechts, 1981). The possession of an elaborate, well-organized information structure distinguishes the expert from the novice. Specific processing advantages, such as a large STM capacity, are not significant factors (Vessey, 1987).

Memory Organization

As the individual interacts with the event world, information is acquired and processed against the prevailing knowledge structure in limited storage memory. If a person's goals, information structures, or environment change, so too will the perception of the event. Processing information may reconfigure the knowledge structure.

The process is evident in programming. As a particular maintenance assignment is carried out for the first time, procedural efficiencies are noted and stored in memory. With each additional performance of the task, other economies are discovered, and cause the knowledge structure to be realigned. The programmer's memory will continue to be updated in this way, and produce an efficient set of procedures for the task. At this stage, the programmer is in possession of a mature memory organization, and is considered an expert.

Experts use certain types of information to recognize and construct programming artifacts (Soloway, 1984; Pennington cited in Vessey, 1987):

1. a large collection of abstract patterns and plans;
2. a moderate assortment of conceptual building blocks; and
3. a small number of programming episodes.

Plans are sets of procedures used by the expert to bring order to programming activity. They are stored in the mind abstractly, and retain only their essential features. As problems are encountered, plans that have produced successful results in like situations are retrieved, combined with other pertinent information, and applied to the problem. Plans fall into the following categories (Soloway, 1984; Bateson, Alexander, & Murphy, 1987).

1. *Strategic plans.* They are employed to achieve the primary objective of the algorithm.
2. *Tactical plans.* They are used to attain a specific objective within the strategic plan, or to solve a problem confined to a section of code.
3. *Implementation plans.* These describe particular ways a programming language can be used to carry out the details of the other plans.

When composing software, the programmer will use an assortment of plans to solve problems. However, solving problems is not the programmer's only concern. It is also important to follow programming conventions. Failure to obey these rules makes an otherwise acceptable program difficult to maintain.

When constructing plans, programmers rely more on previously acquired knowledge than on programming skills (Bateson, Alexander, & Murphy, 1987).

Memory Processing

The keys to efficient processing are to have a robust knowledge network of plans and experiences, and to be able to locate and retrieve the appropriate information to interpret events.

Generally, novices are outperformed by experts because they lack the more sophisticated information resources of the latter. The concepts represented by computer names and the structural significance of code are not as quickly grasped, and much of the information that might have been acquired is lost. When experts scan an instruction sequence, mnemonic names and structures cue memory, and bring into conscious thought information needed to understand the code.

Information retrieval is facilitated when the names and structure of the program correspond to the representation in the maintainer's memory (Vessey, 1987). Data that need to be restructured consume more STM storage and processing resources, are prone to incorrect interpretations, and are very difficult to rectify if a meaningful representation is already stored in memory (Adelson & Soloway, 1984). The information extracted from a program tries to integrate with the existing meaning or semantic network. An inconsistency creates additional processing demands (Mynatt, 1984).

With Respect to Tasks

As software tasks are repeated, efficiencies are learned and become part of the work routine. The techniques used by the expert have been refined many times. The novice is just beginning this process. The performance gap can be narrowed if the novice adopts some of the ways of the expert.

For example, software design is a process where concepts are continually being proposed, changed, and further defined. To keep track of the activity, the expert has learned to make use of a variety of notes that alert the programmer to design assumptions, constraints, and expectations (Soloway, 1984). For debugging software, the expert has strategies to extract information from the program and find errors. He does not try to know the program in detail (Vessey, 1987).

Processing and Storage Limitations

Well-designed software is considerate of the maintainer's processing and storage limitations. Its code is constructed so that information can be efficiently extracted from it. The quicker the program organization and coding functions are understood, the faster and more accurately it will be maintained.

A programmer's limitations are clearly seen in communications theory.

Communications Theory

Communications is the transmission and reception of messages. It is broadly defined here to include all of the means a person may use to affect the thinking of someone else. Communications theory is concerned with these problems (Shannon & Weaver, 1949):

1. *the technical problem*—the accurate transmission of the physical message;
2. *the semantic problem*—the difference between the intended and received meanings of the message; and
3. *the effectiveness problem*—eliciting the desired response from the receiver.

The root cause of much of the difficulty in maintenance is the failure to convey useful information to the programmer. Trouble in assimilating information often happens because the processing limitations of the maintainer have been exceeded. Viewing the programmer as a communications system provides insights into semantic and effectiveness problems.

The information source is where a concept for the program or modification originates. It may be the end user, designer, development programmer, or maintainer.

Messages are the particular ways a concept is expressed. They are sent between each phase of development, and from one maintenance programmer to the next.

The transmission (TX) component converts the message into a form that can be sent through a medium to its destination. With a programmer as the information source, the message is translated into the symbol structure of the programming language for later viewing by a maintainer.

The message is transmitted through the medium. In programming the medium is the compiler listing printout or its display on a screen.

Noise is the distortion that occurs to a message during its transmission through the medium. For a compiler listing, printing that is faded or smudged and screen glare are noise.

The reception (RX) component mirrors transmission. The maintainer uses his eyes to convert the symbols viewed in the compiler listing into an internal representation. The signals are stored temporarily in a buffer (STM).

At the destination, the message is processed using the knowledge structure of the receiver. For the maintenance programmer, that should be a demonstrable understanding of the program's general construction and the functions of its code.

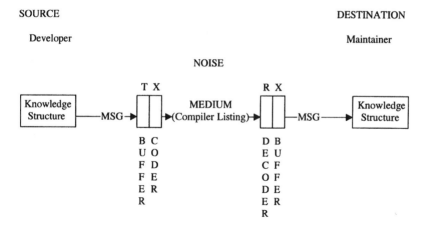

Figure 9. Communications System Model.

A number of messages will be created in the development of a program. Some provide information for the end user, others give direction to the computer operator, and of course the program is written for the maintainer. To communicate effectively, the programmer should take into consideration the conditions in which each message will be employed, and how it will be perceived and utilized at that time. It is not enough to solve the end user's problem. The meaning of variable, routine, and file names, as well as in-program comments, must be assessed within its working context (Kochen, 1984).

Memory Limitations

When messages are received, the text is read and processed against the knowledge structure in memory. How much information is captured is determined by the resources available in STM, and by the robustness of the information network. By cogently structuring messages, the limitations they impose on memory can be lessened.

The relevancy and compatibility of the messages received by the knowledge structure largely determine how restrictive the limitations will be. As symbols are read, the cognitive structures that are associated with them, and the context in which they are used, are activated. If the messages are logically presented and the theme familiar, expectations will be created. They act to facilitate the processing of data that easily fit into the knowledge structure, and inhibit those that do not (Palmer & Jonides, 1988; Pezdek et al., 1989). Features of the items being read are evaluated against information categories. Successful matches are processed automatically, regardless of category length. Irrelevant information cannot be readily assimilated, and creates additional processing demands that degrade performance (Palmer & Jonides, 1988).

If the messages received lack a coherent theme, and require a diverse collection of categories for processing, the facilitating and inhibiting aspects of processing will not be present. As a consequence, information that is pertinent to one's train of thought is absorbed with greater difficulty, and that which is irrelevant considered. Capacity limitations and selecting a focus of attention, that were once insignificant factors, are now major concerns. Unrelated category groupings are more sensitive to the amount of information processed than are ones well learned (Palmer & Jonides, 1988); and, because the ability to semantically categorize information is limited (Mullin & Egeth, 1989) and impaired, increasing the message load causes more processing errors to be committed (Palmer & Jonides, 1988).

Information processing and memory limitations affect complex problem solving and focused memory searches. More resources are consumed to solve complex problems than easy ones (Turner & Engle, 1989), because the semantic structures that would normally be used to facilitate processing have not been developed. Therefore, more space is needed in working memory to store the increased number of times that information awaits disposition. Focused memory searches access well-learned semantic categories. They use a precise and narrowly defined set of parameters for the search that usually retrieves relevant information (Singer, Parbery, & Jakobson, 1988).

Summary

Errors and barriers are nettlesome obstructions in the programming code. The first may be introduced from any of software's development or maintenance stages. Most of the problems that arise can be traced to an errant requirement or design decision. Errors are difficult to correct because programmers must keep track of a number of details, contend with a variety of structures, and not affect other program functions. Barriers are constructions that interfere with a programmer's ability to readily understand programs, locate segments of code, and solve problems. There are five cognitive processes associated with programming: flexibility closure, associative memory, induction, syllogistic reasoning, and spatial scanning.

The information possessed by an expert differs from that of a novice in both quantity and quality. The expert is able to draw upon large organized bodies of knowledge that are structured for efficient recall. The novice's information network is not as developed. He has a tendency to focus on coding details, and therefore creates complex mental representations that are difficult to access.

As symbols are read, the cognitive structures that are associated with them and the context in which they are used are activated. If the messages are logically presented and the theme familiar, expectations will be created. They act to facilitate the processing of data that fit into the knowledge structure, and inhibit those that do not. If the messages received lack a coherent theme, and require a diverse collection of categories for processing, the facilitating and inhibiting aspects of processing will not be present. As a consequence, information that is pertinent to one's train of thought is absorbed with greater difficulty, and that which is irrelevant considered.

Chapter 13
Cognitive Structures

Most programs are large and complex, and their structure helps determine how well they will be maintained (Newsome & Katz, 1987). It is only in small programs that structure has little effect on comprehension and the capacity for modification (Sheil, 1981).

Types of Structure

The traditional way to structure a program is through mathematics and engineering principles (e.g., Couger & Shannon, 1976; Boillot, 1978; Cole, 1978; Dock, 1979; Linger, Mills, & Witt, 1979; Friedman & Koffman, 1981; Hill, 1981). Operations are first broken down into irreducible prime programs, and then collected in a pool to be used for writing applications software. Its programs are characterized by top-down processing, one entry and one exit point, and a minimum number of branching and GOTO statements.

Object-oriented programs are an improvement over traditional structured designs (Isner, 1982; Jacky & Kalet, 1987; Bailin, 1989; Korson & McGregor, 1990). Its programs are developed by defining the entities that exist in the problem space and the relationships that form among them. It produces a structure that closely models the problem state of the end user, and is more maintainable than traditional structured designs. Object-oriented designed programs produce modules that may be used in future modifications, and a structure that can be quickly and accurately expanded.

The techniques proposed significantly improve traditional and object-oriented designs. Both methods rely on language and problem-solving knowledge (Korson & McGregor, 1990). What distinguishes a cognitively structured program from an object-oriented one is the inclusion of information-processing principles and an orientation that looks at not only how the present problem is solved, but also how the maintainers will solve future ones. The method produces software that is easily restructured and less troublesome to correct because the error can be readily localized to the affected section of code (Gould, 1975; Weiser, 1982).

Overview

Structured material is recalled more quickly than a disorganized collection (Mandler & Stein, Mandler & Robinson cited in West & Morris, 1985). When items are part of a visual unit, they acquire spatial properties that are retained along with its content. This information may be later called upon to discriminate among items retrieved by a primary content cue. Order increases the rate at which items are integrated into memory (West & Morris, 1985). Memory can be further enhanced if items are placed in standard structures (Sheil, 1981; Marcus, 1981).

Within a program there are three levels of structure: a global order formed by the interrelationships of modules; a spatial layout of the lines of instructions in a routine; and standard structures for instruction types. They each act to clarify thought and inform the maintainer.

Global Structure

The global structure of a cognitively designed program uses modules that have been created to perform a single function very well (Kernigham & Plauger, 1978). They are designed to be self-contained (Korson & McGregor, 1990). That is, they are able to be modified or deleted without affecting other program functions, and to be understood apart from other code (Kernigham & Plauger, 1978). Details are hidden from the routines that access them (Kernigham & Plauger, 1978; Korson & McGregor, 1990). The module's name and calling arguments should be adequate to describe them, and allow the maintainer to quickly scan the program. Evoking one concept forms a "good gestalt" that is easier to remember than multipurpose ones (Asch et al. cited in Saariluoma & Sajaniemi, 1989).

The program's global structure is seen distinctly when its routines are connected by their calls to one another. Two patterns are normally present. One is a loose collection of processing modules. The other is a hierarchical structure composed of routines that plan, organize, or describe functions. Hierarchical structures facilitate search, especially if they are confined to three or four levels. However, a two-level hierarchy is beneficial, requiring only a minimum of work (Dirlam, 1972), and is easier to process into chunks (Saariluoma & Sajaniemi, 1989).

Spatial Layout of a Routine

The spatial layout of a routine can greatly enhance information processing. Two programs that perform the same computations may impose vastly different cognitive loads on a maintainer's memory (Saariluoma & Sajaniemi, 1989). Code that is convoluted and complex is difficult to comprehend (Chambers, 1983;

Newsome & Katz, 1987), but instructions that have a meaningful structure are readily determined (Newsome & Katz, 1987).

Table 5. Horizontal and Vertical Construction.

	Statement Numbers Columns 1–5	Code Columns 6–59	Comments (gloss) Columns 60–80
Declaration Statements			
Input	1000 series		
User Interface and Dialogue	2000 series		
Iterations and General Code	3000 series 4000 series		
Output	5000 series		
Built-In Diagnostics	6000 series		
Error Processing	7000 series		
Return Processing	8000 series		
Ad Hoc Dumps	9000 series		

Horizontal Layout

The horizontal layout of a FORTRAN program is basically an instruction that includes statement number and instruction fields. Comments, if written, are usually in the same visual space. Both are used to inform the maintainer. Instructions process data, and inform the programmer by the instruction, its structure, and the mnemonics chosen for variables, files, and routines. Comments are written to explain the functions and subtleties of the code. They are useful if well composed, and are particularly valuable when external documentation is missing or faulty. Generally, programs contain only a few comments because a large number of comments obscure the code (DeYoung, Kampen, & Topolski, 1981).

The writer of code needs to communicate to both the novice and expert programmer. The former requires many explanatory comments. The latter needs only a few.

Sending different messages to different people in the same visual space is difficult. However, it can be accomplished by partitioning the horizontal layout. One division is to place the statement numbers in columns 1–5, the code in columns 7–59, and the comments on gloss in columns 60–80. The placement of the comments to the right of the code (e.g., Smith, 1981), as opposed to the left of the statement numbers (Baecker & Marcus, 1986), allows the code to be read without the distraction of unwanted messages, and may be referred to only when additional information is desired (Pinto & Soloway, 1988). Segregating the comments from the code encourages the programmer to describe the processing more fully.

Vertical Layout

A program is easier to understand if the processing order flows unbroken from the top or beginning of the routine to the bottom (Kernigham & Plauger, 1978). Bifurcated sections of code, such as calls to subroutines and IF statements, increase the complexity of a program and make it more difficult to comprehend (Ryge, 1981). They require the programmer to keep track of more items for longer periods of time than code that is sequentially processed.

Software is more easily processed if it is designed in conceptual units, its mnemonics created for maintenance tasks, and its routines structured to accommodate bifurcated processing. One way to achieve this is to partition the processing into tiers, and assign the sections a statement number series. For example, a program might begin with declaration statements, followed by input processing (1000 series), user interface and dialogue processing (2000 series), Do-loops (3000 series) which are normally interposed among general processing (4000 series), output processing (5000 series), error processing (6000 series), built-in diagnostics (7000 series), return processing (8000 series), and ad hoc dumps used in correcting errors (9000 series).

The strata and statement numbers provide additional information to the maintainer at the point of bifurcation (e.g., Smith, 1981). The assigned statement labels act as mnemonic devices (Kernigham & Plauger, 1978). They represent a type of processing, and enable the programmer to immediately discern the function of the section of code that branches out of sequence (Chambers, 1983). Otherwise, the maintainer will be forced to go to that part of the program and study it before a determination can be made. Processing tiers and meaningful statement numbers facilitates closure of thought.

Instruction Formats

Instructions are formatted to clarify their operations and reduce coding errors. They do not need to be complex to benefit from a standard structure. A simple procedure will be coded with fewer syntax errors if it is explicitly structured (Sime, Arblaster, & Green, 1977).

Many programmers write code to conserve space by stringing instruction symbols in a straight line, without intervening blanks. To read such code one must interpret each element, then reassemble them into a more recognizable form (Humphreys, 1987). The additional processing may enhance some cognitive operations (Horton, 1989), but not the ones needed for immediate understanding.

The structures proposed are designed to enhance the performance of the maintenance tasks.

The Subroutine Call Statement

The Subroutine Call Statement directs the processing to an instruction sequence outside the routine. Processing continues in the subroutine until a Return Statement is encountered, causing the processing to revert to the parent routine.

The input and output variables to the subroutine are contained in the Call Statement's argument list. The maintainer is better able to identify the two groups if they are separated by spacing or placed on different lines.

```
CALL MODULE ( INPUT1, INPUT2, INPUT3, OUTPUT )

CALL MODULE ( INPUT1, INPUT2, INPUT3,

             OUTPUT                 )
```

The Read Statement

The input variables of the Read Statement are better understood if each conceptual unit is distinctly represented.

The Common Statement

Blocks of variables are made available to routines through the Common Statement.

Most of the variables should be structured in the common section (Fisher, 1983). One way is to limit each common statement to one variable grouping.

The Arithmetic Statement

In an algebraic expression, the operators are detected first, and provide the loci for cognitive operations (Ranney, 1987). They designate the actions to be performed, and their placement within the equation determines the operation applied to each variable and constant.

The processing of an arithmetic statement is enhanced if its terms are grouped and related to the individual's knowledge structure. The relationships among operators and operands are clearly seen in textbook equations. However, an expression such as

$$W = \frac{X}{X + Y} * (A + B)$$

is often coded as W = (X/(X + Y))*(A + B). The equation can be written as a near textbook expression by varying the spacing and using two instruction lines; for example,

$$W = (\quad X$$
$$/ \ (X + Y))*(A + B)$$

When read quickly, it will be interpreted as such because of the Law of Pregnance.

The Conditional Control (IF) Statement

The Conditional Control Statement is involved in a large portion of errors (Miller, 1974). Its operation is complex. A condition is first evaluated and, depending on the result, processing may be directed to another part of the program (Ryge, 1981). The condition is either an arithmetic or logic expression. The novice processes the logic expression better than the arithmetic one. The experienced programmer exhibits the same proficiency for both expression types. Programmers generally need experience working with it before they can visualize it as a single unit (Shneiderman, 1976).

Logic expressions vary in difficulty. A condition using conjunctive (AND) operations is discerned more readily than one employing the disjunctive (OR), and a positive expression is understood more quickly than a negative (NOT) one. Logic expressions can often be made easier to understand. For example, conditions that combine an OR expression with at least one negative test are error prone, but usually can be restated using an AND expression (Miller, 1974).

The structure of the IF Statement is another factor influencing comprehension and problem solving (Sime, Arblaster, & Green, 1977). The general form of the IF Statement is a condition followed by an executable statement. It is usually coded by linearly stringing together the symbols of the instruction. Recasting the statement to facilitate information processing improves readability (Spencer, 1968) and makes it easier to modify. For example, cognition is enhanced by assigning the conditions, the Boolean operators, and the executable statement to a separate vertical space:

```
IF((X .GT. 0)        .AND.

   (X .LT. 50)       .AND.

   (Z .LT. 100)          ) Y = X + Z
```

Several IF Statements may be used to represent a complex decision. Here too structure is important. The maintainer's ability to understand the function of a decision battery and alter it is affected by whether the processing associated with each IF Statement is nearby (nested) or located beyond the battery (jump). A nested grouping facilitates problem solving for simple decisions, but creates deep embeddings for complex ones. Jumps create large demands for limited resources in short-term memory. For each branch, the maintainer must remember the statement number, and pair it to the processing that occurs there (Sime, Green, & Guest, 1973; Sime, Arblaster, & Green, 1977).

Jumps, however, can be used to represent complex decisions, if they use subroutines or refer to statement numbers that denote processing strata. They enhance problem solving and cause fewer errors because the construction places a minimal load on short-term memory. The information provided by the subroutine or statement number completes the thought, and enables the decision battery to be easily discerned. Decision batteries using informed jumps are simple, employ a standard structure, and therefore are modified with minimal difficulty.

The Iteration (Do-Loop) Statement

An iteration statement repeats instructions. Its instructions are better seen when set apart from other code, such as by indenting the statements as a block (Norcio, 1981) and using a statement number series reserved for iterative instructions (e.g., Smith, 1981).

The Write Statement

The write statement and its format statement are more conducive to maintenance if they approximate the structure seen on the output page. For example, the format statement can be made to reflect the vertical spacing of the output by using single line feed control characters instead of double- and triple-space characters. They will not interfere with horizontal spacing if they are at the left-most part of the instruction.

Documentation

Software is documented to help the maintainer see the function of code and how it relates to other operations. From the documentation the programmer should be able to learn how the software was originally constructed to solve the end user's problem (Brooks, 1981), and what alterations have been made to it.

The Traditional Approach

Programs are traditionally described in external documents, and to a lesser degree in comments interspersed in the code. The programmer uses and maintains each medium differently.

Software is first documented through comments, such as brief introductions to sections of code. They are handy to use and may be revised at the same time the program is altered. They may also obscure the code.

External documentation is intended to provide a complete description of the program. Maintainers generally dislike updating it and do not always perform the task. After a few years, the text will contain a number of discrepancies and will not be used. Furthermore, the information in the document is often in a form the maintainer is unlikely to use, such as flowcharts (Curtis et al., 1989).

A New Approach

Separating comments from instructions permits a more elaborate form of documentation to exist beside the code. It, along with a mnemonic language and other cognitive structures, eliminates the need for an external document. The structure has two advantages over the traditional method. First, the description of the code is situated where it can be conveniently accessed. It is more expedient to glance to one's right for an item of information than to pore through an external text. Second, it is easier to maintain documentation located in one place. Revisions are more likely to be made to documentation positioned next to the code than to an external text.

Documentation Content

Comments are useful if they are well written (Sime, Arblaster, & Green, 1977) and impart new information (Sheil, 1981). They are primarily intended for the maintainer who does not have the background necessary for understanding the code. Knowledgeable programmers have built up a collection of causal relationships and cognitive structures through many interactions with the program. They are able to discern the functions of program segments and relate them to the program's overall plan for solving the end user's problem. The maintainer who is unfamiliar with the software needs additional information to understand difficult sections of code and to make these connections (Pinto & Soloway, 1988).

In developing comments, the programmer needs to be aware of the different information-seeking strategies employed by the maintainer. Information should be provided to the maintainer as needed, and explain the causal interactions that exist between the local section of code and other parts of the program (Pinto & Soloway, 1988).

Documentation Structure

Documentation that is structured and contained within the program is able to immediately satisfy the changing information demands of the maintainer. Those needs are determined in part by the subtask on which he is currently working. For solving nontrivial error correction and modification problems, the maintainer must have a detailed understanding of the program. To locate a section of code, knowledge of the program's structure is required. Knowing how an instruction sequence relates to other parts of the program is important for altering and testing software. The documentor can inform the unknowledgeable programmer in each subtask demand by varying the message content and effectively using the visual space.

Information may be conveyed to the maintainer in several ways. One is an abstract summary of the module at the beginning of the routine. Another is through the titles and headings of processing sections positioned in the instruction sequence. The third is in phrases and short sentences to the right of the code. They describe the processing steps and relate them to other parts of the program. The descriptions are organized into an outline that reflects the processing divisions of the routine.

The size and complexity of the module determine whether the information will be used. Small routines may need only comments to the right of the code. A more complete description is required for large programs.

The type of documentation that has just been read has a bearing on the processing of code. Documentation formats act as advance organizers of thought. Each type primes the maintainer for a different response to the instructions encountered. Messages that are consistent with the structure of the program aid recognition and recall. Inconsistent information causes a more in-depth processing to occur, but can be useful in problem-solving and inference verification situations (Mannes & Kintsch, 1987). Similarly, advanced organizers that use concrete terms are more easily recalled than abstract compositions (Corkill, Bruning, & Glover, 1988). Another factor is the verbosity of the documentation. Succinct expressions are more effective than English prose in coding, error correction, and modification tasks (Sheppard, Kruesi, & Bailey, 1984).

Programs are documented to enhance the maintainer's performance. The summary at the beginning of the routine helps the maintainer solve problems. It should be written in abstract terms, and arrange events in an order that is inconsistent with the program's structure. The processing headings and the outline aid recognition and recall. They need to be expressed in concrete terms (Mayer, 1981).

Titles, headings, and outlines contribute differently to the recognition and recall of code. Titles establish the point of reference used to direct the retrieval process. Headings divide the module into component processes. When encountered, they activate the appropriate context schema for that section of code. Outlines serve to improve the maintainer's knowledge of the routine's organization (Mayer, 1981; Krug et al., 1989).

Summary and Discussion

Complexity and size create a need for structures that elucidate program functions, reveal processing relationships, and help locate sections of code.

Programs may be structured at three levels: global, module, and instruction. The first can be divided into a relational hierarchy of routines that organize events, and a loose collection of procedural routines. The second may be partitioned horizontally to segregate comments from instructions, and vertically into processing strata. Each stratum would be assigned a statement number series. The third can be structured into conceptual chunks to enhance understanding and for easier modification.

Additional information is more useful to a maintainer if it can be found in the compiler listing than in an external document, and is structured to meet the needs of the task at hand. A summary of the module at the beginning of a routine and processing headings interspersed in the instruction sequence help the maintainer solve problems and locate sections of code. Comments to the right of the instructions relate the code to other parts of the program.

The maintainability of a program is difficult to assess using the proposed techniques. They reduce the perceptual complexity of a program through language and structure enhancements. Current measures of program complexity do not consider the processing of information. They are calculated from the instructions and their components, such as Halstead's EFFORT, McCabe's $v(G)$, Woodward's K, Gaffney's Jumps, Chen's MIN, and Benyon–Tinker's Cx (McCabe, 1976; Chen, 1978; Ryge, 1981; Gibson & Senn, 1989). To evaluate a program using the proposed techniques, new measures will be needed that take into account the principles relating to cognition and language (Weyuker, 1988).

Section IV
Implementation and Testing

Chapter 14
Implementing the Solutions

The knowledge gained about software maintenance does little good if it is not applied to the problem. The challenge before the software designer is to use it to craft solutions that meet the changing information demands of the current and future maintainer. The undertaking is difficult because programs, and the environments in which they are used and maintained, have different maintenance needs and must be evaluated separately.

Solutions to maintenance problems may be implemented in either the development or maintenance phase of the software life cycle. Both situations are discussed. The chapter ends by assessing the effectiveness of solutions.

In the Development Phase

Measures to improve maintenance are easier to incorporate into a program during the development phase than after it has been in use. They can and should be implemented in each part of the development process.

Specifications

Specifications that are well thought out to solve the end user's problem form the basis for a maintenance-oriented design. Here, the system's terms and safety concerns are defined. Care should be taken to select names for objects and actions that convey precise, narrow, and congruent meanings. The names provided will eventually be used to create a mnemonic language, and will play a role in forming the global structures of the program. Writing clear unambiguous specifications simplifies the design process.

Design

In the design stage, the specifications are converted into a blueprint for constructing an information system. The design should generate a system that solves the end user's problem and is easy to maintain. A few constraints added to the process will ensure that both goals are met.

The design process is where the requirements are given hardware and software expression, and where safety issues are resolved. The designer must ensure that each task is carried out in the most appropriate mode, that all parts of the system operate in harmony, and that spurious or rare combinations of events do not cause the system to malfunction in ways that harm life or result in financial loss. Hardware must contain physical safeguards to prevent catastrophic failure. Software must also be designed with similar care.

The general structure, operation, and data flow of the program are formed during the software design process. Information about them is conveyed to the implementation programmer through the definitions of routines, variables, and data files. Definitions, and their names, are very important outputs of the design stage. For a routine, they will describe its function, the interfaces needed to interact with other modules in the system, and the contexts in which it will be employed (Rombach, 1991). They may also contain the purpose for which it was created, comment on how it should be incorporated into the program, and note any special features that the routine may have (Gorla, 1991). A description of a variable might include its purpose and function within a specific program. Once accepted, definitions are entered into a software dictionary.

Algorithms can be developed to simplify maintenance. For example, in some programs the bulk of maintenance activity may concern only a few sections of code (Forster & Munro cited in Bennett, 1991). For a program that edits research data (e.g., Smith, 1975), it may be determined that the permissible responses for the variables will change as more is learned about the subject. Recording the response data in an external file that can be codified without affecting the program can accommodate the changes. When the software is executed, the updated file is used to perform editing functions.

Implementation

The implementation stage creates a program from the design. In it modules are laid out spatially, each line of code is structured, and the software is documented. A few routines may also be defined. Maintainability is enhanced if the routines have a low coupling effect and are highly cohesive. That is, their dependency on other routines is minimized, and there is a large degree of interaction among the instructions (Gorla, 1991). To reduce the number of errors that will be committed, the routines and the subsystems should be kept small (Gorla, 1991).

Checkout

The checkout stage is where the program is tested for compliance with the specifications. It is the last chance to make sure it is properly structured for maintenance before it is turned over to the end user.

In the Maintenance Phase

Programs that have been in use for a number of years are valuable. They may contain information essential for the operation of an organization, such as its rules, its goals, and important business decisions. Although inefficient and difficult to maintain, they cannot simply be discarded or replaced with either an off-the-shelf software package or rewritten system (Bennett, 1991).

Restoring the program offers a way to preserve valuable corporate information, and may nearly achieve a level of maintainability of a newly developed program.

Table 6. The Software Dictionary for an Engine Fuel Flow System.

Rules for Mnemonic Construction
AAAANN—Index structure; 4-character mnemonic stem followed by a 2-character digit.
AAABBB—Bigram structure; two 3-character mnemonics.
Verb*Object—A bigram structure having a verb mnemonic in the first position, followed by a modifier or noun mnemonic representing the object.
Modifier*Noun—A bigram structure using a modifier in the first position to further define the noun in the second position.
AAADDD—A matrix structure with a 3-character mnemonic stem in the first three positions, and three single character descriptors in the last three positions.
Mnemonic Definitions
Index Structure
DUMP__—Displays the variables and constants pertinent to a section of code.
01—Dumps all control values.
02—Dumps all data values.
Bigram Structure
MEA___—Modifier; refers to a measurement taken from a gauge.
Descriptor Matrix
C__—Calculation; a value derived from other data; belongs to the descriptor set that indicates the data's source (C, M).

The Decision

Software is restored for different reasons. Some of these factors are (Bennett, 1991) as follows.

- A large maintenance assignment has been received for the program.
- The cost of maintaining it is excessive.

- The program has been upgraded in status or in strategic importance.
- Knowledge of how to improve software maintenance has been acquired.
- Maintenance procedures have been reevaluated and changed.

The Restoration

Restorations vary in scope and substance. They may involve only a few sections of code or affect the entire program.

One effective restoration is to restructure the software into a top-down hierarchy of modules and use structured programming techniques to improve the readability of the code (Gorla, 1991). In a restructuring, all program transformations are carried out within the same level of abstraction, and the external behavior of the initial program is retained (Bennett, 1991).

A more radical restoration is re-engineering. Here, software engineering principles are used to modify the code and the data files. Over a period of time, it will be more cost effective to re-engineer an existing program to accommodate modifications than to redevelop the software (Gorla, 1991).

Program Improvements

Because of sloppy maintenance practices and poor initial designs, old programs have a tendency to be cumbersome and inefficient. They can be made to operate faster. The following improvements (Arthur, 1988) may be implemented at the same time the software is being restored.

1. Place outside of the Do-loop, the instructions that initialize variables or that need to be performed only once.
2. End Do-loop execution as soon as possible.
3. Minimize the time required to search through a table by ordering its items according to their probability of being matched.
4. Ensure that subexpressions are calculated only once.
5. Wherever possible, replace algorithms with ones that are more efficient, and that retain or better the current level of maintainability.
6. Restructure program data to minimize input and output processing.
7. Ensure that numeric data are placed into the most appropriate format.
8. Eliminate all unneeded data conversions.

Planning

Plans are needed to ensure that the restorations are carried out as intended. Their complexity will vary in accordance with the extent and nature of the revision. Most will require the programmer to make several passes through the code before the software is fully restored. An example of such a plan is the following (Arthur, 1988).

First pass. Visually structure the routines, and make the instruction sequence more readable. Place comments and instructions into separate column areas. Insert blank comment lines between instructions. Cognitively structure each line of code.

Second pass. Redesign the program's IF and Do-loop statements. Try to replace negative and disjunctive logic with expressions that are stated positively and that use the conjunctive operation. Use statement numbers in the 3000 series for Do-loops. Add comments.

Third pass. Partition the instruction sequence into processing layers, and use a different statement number series for each stratum. Delete extraneous code. Insert headings to sections of code. Add comments.

Fourth pass. Analyze and modify the algorithm for clarity and efficiency. Ensure that subexpressions are calculated only once. Try to eliminate data conversions. Make sure that each routine represents only one concept, and develop a summary of its function. Add comments.

Fifth pass. Redesign input and output processing to aid cognition. Structure the formats of write statements to reflect the output page. Group the variables in common statements into conceptual units. Add comments.

Sixth pass. Develop and implement a language of mnemonics for the names given to variables, routines, and files. Record the language in a software dictionary.

At the completion of each pass, the program should be tested briefly to determine if any errors have been introduced into the system. A more rigorous testing will be conducted at the conclusion of the restoration to make certain the program still conforms to the specifications.

Assessing Effectiveness

Software that has been recently created or restored needs to be evaluated to ensure that the maintenance problems originally identified are solved, and that new impediments have not been introduced. Comparing the program's maintenance and performance record to the historical standard assesses the effectiveness of the restoration. The comparison needs to consider the maintainability of the software making up the standard. If the programs had not been designed for maintenance, their restoration should result in significantly lower completion times for maintenance assignments. If not, the programmer must find out why. Perhaps the maintainer needed more time to learn the new system, or the information was inadequate. For restructured programs in the standard, the difference should be slight.

Statistics that a programmer may want to keep are the type and difficulty of the maintenance tasks, the level of expertise of the programmer at the time the task was carried out, the size and complexity of the program, and the time required to perform certain functions.

Summary

Measures to solve maintenance problems may be implemented in either the development or maintenance phase of the software life cycle.

It is easier to provide for maintenance during the program's development than after it has been written. Each stage of development affects maintainability: the specifications provide definitions that convey precise, narrow, congruent meanings; the design produces a clear unambiguous blueprint for constructing software; the implementation converts the design into a maintainable program; and the checkout ensures that all maintenance provisions have been incorporated into the code.

For old software, a plan should be devised to restore code near the maintainability of a newly developed program. It should also contain procedures to increase the program's operating efficiency.

Software that has been recently created or restored needs to be evaluated to ensure that the problems originally identified are solved, and that new impediments have not been introduced.

Chapter 15
Testing

Software is tested to ensure it satisfies the end user's requirements (Rubey cited in Chudleigh, 1990), operates with other programs in the system, and is safe (i.e., it will not harm people or cause financial loss). Affecting the process is its construction (Laprie, 1990). A program that is easily understood and designed for maintenance stands a better chance of being free of errors than one lacking these traits (Chudleigh, 1990). But no matter how well thought out the design, or how thorough the testing, errors may remain in the code (Dijkstra quoted in Chudleigh, 1990).

Testing is time consuming and expensive. To remove all software errors requires that each path through the program be examined for each input and environment combination that can occur. Usually it is not practical to test software completely (Chudleigh, 1990; Parnas, van Schouwen, & Kwan, 1990). The end user may receive the program if it generally operates as intended and most of its errors have been corrected. Safety-critical code, of course, is tested more thoroughly. It is helpful in testing to have safety-critical code isolated from other program functions, and to keep its design small and simple (Parnas, van Schouwen, & Kwan, 1990).

Software needs to be tested in the environment in which it will be used. Contrived situations are mere abstractions of its intended milieu, and contain an unknown quantity of errors and distortions (Chudleigh, 1990; Parnas, van Schouwen, & Kwan, 1990).

Hardware and Software Testing

The reliability of an information system depends on how well its hardware and software have been tested. The same procedures used confidently to test hardware are applied to software. Because the components are fundamentally different, this practice is questioned.

Hardware

The procedures for testing hardware are developed from experiences in building physical systems. A physical design may be refined many times and reaches a point where its remaining errors can be discounted (Leveson, 1990; Parnas, van

Schouwen, & Kwan, 1990). System reliability is defined by equations that factor in the random fault rates of its components, and is published (Chudleigh, 1990; Leveson, 1990; Parnas, van Schouwen, & Kwan, 1990).

Software

Unlike hardware, software failures are systematic failures caused by a faulty specification or design (Thomas, 1990). In assessing its reliability, the complete finished product needs to be used without regard to the processes used to create it (Parnas, van Schouwen, & Kwan, 1990), or its components. Module reliability cannot be accurately measured (Chudleigh, 1990). Getting routines to work together creates problems that are more difficult to solve than in hardware, and is often complex. These various problems make it nearly impossible to develop a failure rate model (Leveson, 1990).

Software Testing Overview

Testing is conducted throughout the program's life cycle to ensure that the intended specifications are met. The tests may be static or dynamic.

Static Testing

Static tests are inspections. They may be performed on any well-defined product of the development or maintenance stage (e.g., specifications, program design, code, or test plan), and at different levels of formality. Inspections are less expensive than dynamic tests.

The Informal Review. In an informal review, or desk check, the programmer who created the product performs the inspection. He may scan the compiler listing for errors, hand check the calculations, or manually simulate program functions to check on the logic and data flow (Glass, 1979).

The Walk-Through. A committee of other programmers evaluates the product in a walk-through. They examine the product in detail to ensure it is error free and properly structured. For a software design, the walk-through is called a design review; for code, a program logic review (Glass, 1982).

The Fagan Inspection. A Fagan inspection also utilizes an evaluation committee of programmers to examine the product. However, its meetings are formal, and the inspection is more thorough. Prior to the meeting, copies of the product and support literature are distributed to the inspectors to study. If the product is code, the meeting's agenda is to go over each instruction, and determine its validity. A secretary takes minutes of the proceedings, and records each error found (Russell, 1991). Fagan inspections are effective. They detect errors up to four times faster than dynamic testing. Each hour the program is inspected reduces the maintenance effort by an average of 33 hours (Russell, 1991).

The causes of errors discovered through inspections are self-evident and are easy to correct. The programmer needs only to edit the code. Dynamic tests, in contrast, uncover the symptoms, and require additional effort to detect and rectify the errant code (Russell, 1991).

Inspections complement dynamic testing. They reveal anomalous code that is very difficult to uncover otherwise. For example, extra statements may never be found through dynamic testing, and omitted instructions are difficult to find if they occur in seldom used paths of the program (Russell, 1991).

Dynamic Testing

Software is dynamically tested to ensure that it operates properly. The tests are designed to expose errors in program execution, timing, and system interaction, and prepare the product for end user acceptance (Russell, 1991).

Dynamic tests may be performed with or without knowledge of the routine's internal operation. The latter, functional or black-box tests, uses different input combinations to determine if the program produces the output intended by the specifications. Structural or white-box tests are designed to exercise only the code segment thought to be in error (Ould & Unwin, 1986; Chudleigh, 1990; Russell, 1991).

Functional Tests

Random Input. A random input test uses a randomly chosen subset of the possible input value combinations (Omar & Mohammed, 1991). It works better on small programs than on large programs. How well it performs depends on the distribution of input values (Marick, 1990).

Equivalence Partitioning. Equivalence partitioning uses representatives of data groupings to test the program. The possible responses for a variable are divided into nonoverlapping valid and invalid classes (e.g., day of the week: less than 1 = invalid; 1–7 = valid; greater than 7 = invalid). Every datum within a class is assumed to be processed the same way. Therefore, only one value within the class needs to be tested (Ould & Unwin, 1986; Omar & Mohammed, 1991).

Boundary-Value Analysis. Boundary-value analysis searches for program errors at the equivalence class borders. The test is used on both input and output data, and complements equivalence partitioning (Ould & Unwin, 1986).

Cause–Effect Graphing. Cause–effect graphing develops test cases from the causes and effects identified in the specifications. The relationships of input condition causes to output effects are described by Boolean operations, and are pieced together to form the cause–effect graph. The graph is easily constructed for small programs, but as software grows, the graph increases in size and soon becomes unmanageable. Large graphs need to be converted to decision tables, and have equivalence partitioning and boundary-value analysis applied to them before being used as test data. The graph may be used to uncover specification deficiencies (Ould & Unwin, 1986; Omar & Mohammed, 1991).

The Condition Table Method. Condition combinations found primarily in the specifications are used to test the program. The method's focus is on how data should be processed (Omar & Mohammed, 1991).

The Category-Partition Method. The category-partition method examines the program in functional units, and is particularly well suited to test complex software systems. Its test cases are developed from the different functions in the specifications. The input parameters of the functions are defined by their characteristics (i.e., categories), partitioned into equivalence classes (i.e., choices), and constrained to reflect their usage in the specifications. Test data are selected from the constrained choices (Omar & Mohammed, 1991).

Structural Tests

Statement Testing. Each statement is tested to ensure that it is able to be executed (Jeng & Weyuker, 1989; Weyuker & Jeng, 1991). Statement and branch testing are included in all software test plans (Dyer & Kouchakdjian, 1990).

Branch Testing. Branch testing is used primarily to determine if each instruction branch can be accessed (Dyer & Kouchakdjian, 1990). It is better suited for detecting path selection faults caused by errant relational operators, variable references, and constants, than for computational errors (Girgis cited in Marick, 1990). It also does not do well on programs containing loops (Ntafos cited in Marick, 1990). Branch and statement testing are rudimentary error searches, and need to be supplemented with path testing to verify programs (Dyer & Kouchakdjian, 1990).

Path Testing. Path testing traverses each trail through the program, from entry to exit (Jeng & Weyuker, 1989; Weyuker & Jeng, 1991). It is a more thorough examination than either statement or branch testing (Marick, 1990; Dyer & Kouchakdjian, 1990).

Data Flow Testing. Data flow testing is a special form of path testing (Marick, 1990). It uses different combinations of variable definitions and values to exercise program paths (Jeng & Weyuker, 1989; Weyuker & Jeng, 1991). In large and complex software, the number of test cases generated is more than can be practically examined (Dyer & Kouchakdjian, 1990).

Test Plans

The test plan's methods and procedures verify that the program meets the specifications. All of its tests and inspections, regardless of where they are applied in the program's life cycle, refer back to the requirements and specifications. Specifications that are well written reduce the number of errors committed throughout the project and facilitate the development of a test plan.

Plans vary in complexity. For small programs, used only by their author, the plan may be simply to casually inspect the code. If the software is large and complex, written for public use, and capable of harming people or causing financial loss, a more thorough testing will be needed.

An example of a test plan is Harlan Mills's "clean room" testing for software development. Independent testers perform all testing. The programmers who created the software are not permitted to execute it, and therefore must write the program carefully. The testers check the program with randomly generated cases, and send both the tests and their results to the program developer's supervisor. The method produces a product that is more reliable than when the authors test their creation (Parnas, van Schouwen, & Kwan, 1990).

All test plans are imperfect, and will leave errors in the system.

Life Cycle Testing

Tests may be conducted at each stage of the program's life cycle.

Specifications

Specifications can be developed with knowledge extraction methods (e.g., specification animation, knowledge-based systems, and rapid prototyping) that record thoughts precisely in a computational form, and in sufficient detail to confirm the end user's intent (Chudleigh, 1990).

For safety-critical specification segments, finite state machines, decision tables, decision trees, and Petri nets are used to detect errors and potential problems.

Finite State Machines. A finite state machine is an abstract mechanism used to represent a series of transformations. The machine consists of a finite input alphabet (I), a finite set of states (S), and a finite output alphabet (O). At each frame of time ($t = 0, 1, \ldots, n$), the machine reacts to input stimuli (I_t) to produce an output ($f(I_t, S_t) = O_t$) and the next machine state ($f(I_t, S_t) = S_{t+1}$) (Gill, 1962; Parnas, van Schouwen, & Kwan, 1990; Omar & Mohammed, 1991).

Decision Tables. When a finite state machine becomes too complicated to understand, a decision table may be used to model the system. The table is essentially a collection of condition–action rules. The rules form the columns. The conditions of the system are in the first set of rows; the actions that may be triggered follow. Rules are defined by the conditions and actions they require to be present. Sometimes rules overlap (i.e., require the same condition state, and either the same or different actions), becoming either redundant or inconsistent (Moret, 1982). The table may be used to organize the specifications.

Decision Trees. Decision trees are binary trees that structure information much like a decision table. The nodes of the tree represent the system's conditions, and the two branches from each node, the condition's presence or absence. At the leaf nodes are the actions required to be performed. Each path through the tree is a rule (Moret, 1982; Omar & Mohammed, 1991).

Table 7. A Decision Table.

	Rule 1	Rule 2	Rule 3	Rule 4
Condition 1	Absent	Present	Present	Present
Condition 2		Absent	Present	Present
Condition 3	Present	Present		Absent
Action 1	Do			
Action 2		Do		
Action 3				Do
Action 4			Do	

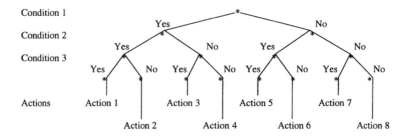

Figure 10. A Decision Tree.

Petri Nets. Petri nets are similar to flow charts. They use circles to represent places, bars for transitions, and directed arcs to connect places to transitions and transitions to places. Markers, or tokens, keep track of the execution flow. As a place or transition is fired, a token(s) is advanced to the next juncture(s) in the system. Places and transitions must have tokens on all of their inputs to execute (Peterson, 1977). Petri nets are used to represent parallel or concurrent programs, and systems that must be precisely and unambiguously defined (Peterson, 1977; Omar & Mohammed, 1991).

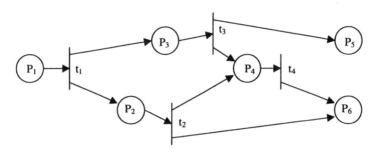

Figure 11. A Petri Net.

Design

Designs are tested for conformity to the specifications, and how well they address software construction and maintenance issues. Some concerns are as follows.

1. The design should allow program components to be independently constructed and modified.
2. Module interface definitions should be precise and unambiguous.
3. There should be no duplicate functions.
4. The routines should work together as a system.

To help construct the design, the programmer may elect to use a program design language (PDL). A PDL is a constrained language that employs certain key words and phrases to describe software structures (e.g., If a Then b Else c; Do f While n) (Linger, Mills, & Witt, 1979; Basili & Mills, 1982; Curtis et al., 1989; Omar & Mohammed, 1991).

Implementation

Implementation testing makes certain the algorithms developed in the design stage are correctly put into code, and the instructions meet the specifications. The form of testing is inspection (Parnas, van Schouwen, & Kwan, 1990).

"Suspicion testing" is a partition-testing strategy well suited for the implementation stage. Components are selected for testing if they are likely to fail, such as the following.

1. They were coded by a novice or marginally skilled programmer.
2. They have been restructured late in the design or implementation stage.
3. The programmer lacks confidence in their construction.
4. They have a history of problems.

Each tester may have additional reasons for inspecting routines (Hamlet & Taylor, 1990).

Checkout

Programs in checkout are tested in isolation, and as they function in the software system and finished software-hardware product. Success at testing can be determined through mutation analysis. Mutations, or errors, are randomly interjected into the program prior to testing. After testing, the errors found are evaluated in relation to the undetected mutations. Mutation analysis assumes a "competent programmer" and the "coupling effect." That is, the program is nearly error-free, and a test that reveals simple errors will also detect complex mistakes (Adrion, Branstad, & Cherniavsky, 1982; Howden, 1982). Mutation testing is very costly (Marick, 1990).

There are many testing strategies that require the program to be run. One that does not is symbolic execution. The test exercises the program, one path at a time. Each assignment statement contains a variable to the left of the equal sign that is defined in terms of a symbolic expression to its right. Whenever that variable is subsequently referenced, the symbolic expression is used in its place. The symbolic execution of the following code (Table 8) illustrates the technique.

```
READ A, B

A = A + 1

B = B + A + 1

C = A - B

IF (A = B) A = B + C

A = B - C

END
```

Drawbacks to symbolic execution are the combinatorial explosion that occurs if all paths through the program are considered, CALL statement processing, determining path feasibility, and validating a path expression (Adrion, Branstad, & Cherniavsky, 1982; Howden, 1982; Zelkowitz, 1990; Coward, 1991).

Table 8. A Symbolic Execution Table.

Path	Condition	A	B	C
READ A, B				
A=A+1		A+1		
B=A+B			A+B+1	
C=A-B+1				(A+1-(A+B+1)+1
				B+1
IF (A=B)	(A+1)=(A+B+1)			
Branch 1				
Branch 2				
		Branch 1		
A=B+C		(A+B+1)+(B+1)		
		A+2B+2		
		Branch 2		
A=B-C		(A+B+1)-(B+1)		
		A		

Integration testing assesses how well the program interacts with other software components in the system. At the design stage, integration testing was performed by inspection. In checkout, the program is executed with the software system. The testing begins with a small group of modules. If the routines are compatible, additional programs are included in the aggregate, and the testing continues. The process ends when the software system operates within tolerances (Ould & Unwin, 1986).

System testing evaluates the program under realistic conditions. That is, it and all of the software and hardware components are tested as a functional unit within the environment that is likely to be encountered. For safety-critical situations, the program's reliability must be known before it can be put to use. One way of determining reliability is through random testing. Its test cases are randomly sampled from the set of possible input configurations (Parnas, van Schouwen, & Kwan, 1990). Random testing is very effective on small programs (Marick, 1990).

Maintenance

Programs must be tested every time they are modified or corrected. Reexaminations, or regression testing, need to check out only the sections of code that the alterations affect.

Generally, the same test cases employed in checkout are used, although some adjustments may be made (Adrion, Branstad, & Cherniavsky, 1982).

Discussion

Programs that are designed for maintenance are well suited for testing. Both are performed best on software that is readily understood and can be decomposed into functional units. Specifications and the design need to be clearly expressed. The sooner an error can be detected, the less costly it will be to correct. Black- and white-box testing are also simplified. A well-structured program can be examined more effectively than an unprincipled design, and will confine errors to smaller sections of the code (Adrion, Branstad, & Cherniavsky, 1982).

Section V
Concluding Remarks

Chapter 16
Concluding Remarks

Designing maintainable software requires looking at programs and programming from the perspective of one about to alter the code. It is more than writing understandable code. It is a change in attitude that affects many decisions in the computer department. Making the computer efficient is still important. Only now it is weighed against the impact it has on maintenance.

One decision affecting maintenance is the choice of a programming language. Expressive languages, that have a large and varied instruction set, give the development programmers many ways to write an algorithm, but can be difficult for the maintainer to quickly interpret. A better choice is a language that allows a process to be written in only one way.

Another is the selection of programmers. The criterion most widely used is knowledge of a specific programming platform (i.e., computer, operating system, programming language, etc.). But this can be picked up easily on the job, and is not as important to maintenance as, for example, knowing how people of varying skills learn and communicate. What programmers must excel in is organizing thought and creating abstract mechanisms to process data.

The choice of manager is an important decision. Managers set goals, establish and maintain values, and solve organizational and technical problems. They should possess good technical training and a history of applying that knowledge to software projects. Motivators, cheerleaders, and accountants do not contribute significantly to software maintenance or the computer department.

Appendices

Appendix A
The Information Age

Software maintenance affects information and the information age in which we are now living. It is information that drives our complex society. It enables both the individual and the corporation to function as part of a community. Information is vital to a human being. It even has been argued that to have life is to have the ability to receive, process, and communicate information (Debons, Horne, & Cronenweth, 1988). Information is certainly indispensable to a head of state who must direct and interact with several departments of government including the military. Airlines rely on information to develop schedules that minimize the time a traveler will spend in an airport waiting for a connecting flight. Information also provides flight attendants and travel agents with the means to make a passenger's trip more enjoyable (e.g., the weather at the destination, the gate number of the passenger's connecting flight, points of interest along the way, etc.). Managers of inventories employ information to more efficiently acquire raw materials and distribute finished products. Its importance can be seen in the automobile industry's "just-in-time" inventory system where cars are assembled using components that arrive as needed, or within a department store in which management uses point-of-sale data to replenish stocks and purchase additional merchandise. The more effectively we use information as individuals or as organizations, the more valuable we are to society.

The effects of software and its maintenance are not restricted to an individual or company. Through the exchange of information, societies of the world are becoming globally integrated. A network of computers and telecommunications equipment now interconnects the world, enabling distant communities to interact and work together. News events in faraway places are routinely seen as they occur via television. Business is less and less confined to a geographical location. An automobile may be designed in Italy, manufactured in Japan, and sold in the United States. Global ventures are rapidly becoming the norm. However, as people and companies around the world reach out to one another, as their lives and well being become more interdependent, they become increasingly reliant on systems that generate and distribute information. Such systems depend on well-maintained software.

Appendix B
Information Systems

The information age emerged through the widespread use of sophisticated information systems. Such systems increase our ability to process data, and enable individuals, communities, and societies to interact. Telephones, cable television, robots, facsimiles, and personal computers are examples of information systems we all use or know. Through them we are able to participate in the information age.

Many of the functions performed by information systems would be impossible without the computer. The computer is the principal component in systems that monitor the performance of automobile engines, route messages through telecommunications networks to their proper destination, and simulate the diagnostic abilities of an internist. Without the computer modern information systems would either not be able to be created or would operate with fewer features.

The computer is a remarkable machine. It is able to perform many roles, and even has fooled some people into believing it was a human being (Weizenbaum, 1976). Its versatility stems from the ability of its circuitry (hardware) to be modified by a series of instructions (software). Although both work together as a unit, their nature and characteristics are quite different. Understanding hardware and software show how information systems are able to operate, and point to how each can be maintained.

Hardware

The computer is an assembly of electronic components (the physical machine) that is structured according to a system of logical rules (the logic machine). The physical machine is described in terms of electric and magnetic energy patterns that obey well-known and predictable laws of physics. But what makes a computer valuable is that it functions according to a system of logic rules. It is the logic machine that manipulates the symbols we use, and distributes them to remote locations. These rules of logic are also well known and operate in ways that are understood. The logic machine is structured in a hierarchy. At the lowest level are AND-gates, OR-gates, inverters, flip-flops, and the like. They are used to construct arithmetic-logic units, multiplexers, and address decoders at higher levels. At the top level are machine instructions that govern the computer's operations. Computers and other equipment used in information systems are designed first as logic machines. It is at this level that they are understood (Winograd & Flores, 1986).

Software

Software, or programs, is a collection of instruction sequences written to control the action of a computer. It transforms a general-purpose machine into one created for a specific function. The economy that software gives computers accounts, in part, for their widespread use. New computers do not have to be designed and manufactured every time additional processing requirements arise. Only the program needs to be modified.

Programs are composed of symbols. Some represent arithmetic, logic, and other functions of the computer. Others correspond to expressions in an applications domain. Writing software, or programming, is the act of sequencing computer operations, for use on an array of variables from an applications domain, to achieve a desired result. Software turns the computer into a specialized symbol processor.

The symbols used to write software are composed within the rules and structure of a programming language. Languages range from those that closely represent the logic operations of the computer to ones more appropriate for use in the event world. Assembler languages, which are developed from machine languages, are examples of the former. They are used to describe the computer because they are able to depict the stepwise execution of a series of instructions. Each operation of the computer (e.g., comparison, multiplication, addition, etc.) corresponds to a command in an assembler language. At the next level are high-order languages, the languages in which most software is written (e.g., FORTRAN, COBOL, and LISP) (Winograd & Flores, 1986).

Although software operates by the computer's rules of logic, there is little guidance and few reliable rules for extracting a set of variables from an applications domain and manipulating them in an intended way. This presents many problems for software developers and maintainers, and is a factor contributing to software failures.

Appendix C
Software Failures

Software does not always operate as the developer, maintainer, or end user had envisioned. Processing errors are often introduced into the instruction sequence. Some may be inconsequential. Others will have a debilitating effect.

Society's dependence on a flow of timely and accurate information is most apparent when that flow is suddenly interrupted or becomes faulty. The excerpt below, from a study by Tom Forester and Perry Morrison (1990), recounts a number of computer and information system failures.

> But most computer malfunctions are created by software failure of one kind or another. Aerospace, the military and space travel provide many such examples. For instance, when USAF pilots were testing the F-16 fighter aircraft, the first thing they did was to tell the onboard computer to raise the landing gear while the plane was still on the runway. Scratch one very expensive F-16. In 1987 another F-16 stalled and plummeted into the Gulf of Mexico because the onboard computer was not programmed to cope with very slow flying. And in another military incident, an F/A-18 attempted to launch a wing-tip missile, but although it was correctly ignited, the computer failed to release the restraining clamp. Thus the hapless pilot found an extra 3000 lbs. of thrust on one wing-tip. In other well-known software snafus, an Atlas-Aegena rocket blasted off from Cape Canaveral en route to Venus, but had to be blown up after it went crazy because a single hyphen had been left out of the flight path program; the loss of the Mariner 18 space probe was found to be due to a one-line programming error, while the USSR lost its Phobos I Mars probe in a similar way.

> Medical computer glitches have also caused the loss of many lives. In 1980, a man undergoing microwave arthritis therapy was killed when the therapy reprogrammed his pacemaker, while faulty software in an insulin infusion pump caused insulin to be delivered at the wrong rates and a patient monitoring system was recalled after it was discovered that it had mixed up patients' names and records. The future health of the world may also have been damaged by design errors in the programs aboard NASA observation satellites

during the 1970s and 1980s. The programs rejected the ozone readings registered over Antarctica at that time, because they were so low and were therefore regarded as spurious. The deviations from normal levels were so extreme that they were assumed to be errors. It was only when UK scientists using ground-based instruments reported that a decline in ozone levels was occurring that NASA scientists reprocessed their data going back to 1979 and confirmed the UK finding (Forester & Morrison, 1990, p. 464).

Philip Elmer-Dewit (1990) reported that in January 1990, A. T. & T. experienced a breakdown in their long distance telephone network because of a single logic error. That mistake cost the company from $60,000,000.00 to $75,000,000.00. He also recounted other failures.

> To experts who track technology mishaps, the past decade reads like an unending parade of computer disasters, ranging from the humiliating bugs that delayed one space shuttle launch after another to the Belgian stock-exchange computers that collapsed under the rush of sell orders during last October's minicrash. Computerized elevator doors have shut unexpectedly. Factory robots have started without warning, killing workers. A misprogrammed medical X-ray machine delivered fatal doses of radiation to at least three cancer patients (Elmer-Dewit, 1990, p. 58–59).

Appendix D
Problem Solving

The initial thought that registers with most people with regard to problem solving is that it is difficult. If pressed for a definition one might respond by saying that it is a series of steps that is pursued to resolve some troubling situation. It would have a beginning (a problem situation has been determined to exist, and a solution is sought to eliminate it), a middle (the problem is defined, various solutions are proposed, and the candidate showing the most promise is chosen for implementation), and an end (the proposed solution is tried, and is tested for effectiveness).

However, this would not be an accurate depiction of the process. Problem solving is actually much more involved, and it proceeds in a nonlinear fashion. In some situations it may be advantageous to add or restructure a step. For example, the problem definition step can be broken down into defining the problem state, describing the problem domain, and defining the solution state components. For other situations, a step may become unnecessary. If only one solution candidate has been proposed, there is obviously no need to select one from a collection of alternatives. For each problem encountered, the appropriateness of the standard procedures should be assessed, and if warranted, be altered to fit the present situation. The sequence in which these procedures are actually performed differs from what is generally expected (i.e., a sequential processing of problem steps). A monotonic order of processing exists only for the simplest cases. For complex problems, such as those faced in programming, steps that have been performed may be reexamined as new insights into the problem are gained. Procedures are often repeated several times. A solution is achieved when a detailed path from the initial problem state to a desired solution state has been found. Problem solving is complicated and difficult (Polya, 1957).

Appendix E
Software Science

Maurice Halstead's system of metrics is derived from the number of operators and operands contained in a program (Fitzsimmons & Love, 1978; Halstead, 1979; Coulter, 1983). Using these counts he described and characterized software. Halstead called the grand total of operators and operands appearing in a program, the program's length.

$N = N_1 + N_2$ where: N is the program's length;
                                     N_1 is the total number of operators;
                                     N_2 is the total number of operands.

The program's vocabulary he defined as the total number of unique operators and operands.

$N = n_1 + n_2$ where: n is the program's vocabulary;
                                     n_1 is the number of unique operators;
                                     n_2 is the number of unique operands.

A more complex measure is the volume of a program. It purports to measure the number of mental comparisons that a programmer makes when writing a program of length N. A search through a binary tree is assumed.

$V = N \log_2 n.$

Equivalent programs (i.e., programs that perform the same task) may have different volumes due to dissimilarities in the algorithms they employ. The most succinct algorithm has the potential volume of V^*. V^* is calculated using the name of the routine and those in the parameter list. For V^* algorithms, the program's length and vocabulary are equal, and the number of operators is 2. One operator is the routine's name. The other is the grouping name separating the routine's name from the parameter list.

$V^* = (2 + n_2{}^*) \log_2 (2 + n_2{}^*)$ where: V^* is the potential volume;
                                               2 is the number of operators;
                                               n_2 is the number of operands (i.e., the parameters).

The implementation level (L) of a given program is obtained by comparing the potential volume to the actual volume. As the length of a program approaches its vocabulary, the implementation level nears unity.

$L = V*/V$.

For programs lacking a parameter list, such as compilers, the potential volume cannot be calculated using the preceding equation. To determine the implementation level in these cases, an approximation is used.

$L = 2/n_1 * n_2/N_2$.

The amount of effort required to implement a program (E) increases in proportion to the routine's size, and decreases as its algorithm becomes more efficient. The following equation takes both of these factors into account.

$E = V/L$

Another metric is the calculation of the time needed to implement a program. It is determined by dividing the implementation effort by the number of elementary mental discriminations made in a second (S). A psychologist named John Stroud (1955) has suggested that S lie somewhere between 5 and 20. In Halstead's experiments the best results occurred when S was set to 18.

$T = E/S$ where: T is the implementation time;
E is the implementation effort;
S is the Stroud number (18).

Appendix F
Sensory Input Processing

Our awareness of the external world begins when the sensory receptors within our bodies become excited by outside stimuli. The receptors transform these excitations into nerve impulses and send them on to the brain where they are processed. The brain sorts through the data received, rejects most, but channels a portion to short-term memory (STM) to become conscious thought.

STM is also called working memory (Schneider & Detweiler, 1987; Waldrop, 1987; Klapp & Netick, 1988; Turner & Engle, 1989). It is characterized by storage that is restricted to a capacity of approximately $7\pm$ items (Miller, 1956) or possibly as few as 4 (Simon, 1969), and to a duration of about 30 seconds unless the time is refreshed through rehearsal. Items processed for a lengthier retention are recorded as long-term memory (LTM).

The working capacity of STM is increased if the input data are structured to access LTM. That is, if the items are organized into chunks. Chunks are conceptual units residing in LTM. They are formed when items become recognized as a unit (Simon, 1969). Chunks are accessed and brought into STM when an item that can be associated with them is processed in working memory. The item in STM cues the chunk in LTM.

STM storage capacity is affected by distractions and from interference caused by items competing for attention (Simon, 1969; Klapp, 1987).

Appendix G
EATPUT Model of the Vision System

Within our general information processing system, the vision system functions as an acquisition component. It senses objects and actions in the event world, and conveys a representation of them to the processing component. However, if the vision system is examined separately, another EATPUT system can be seen. The components of sight form a miniature information system (Grusser & Grusser-Cornehls, 1986; Gregory, 1990).

1. *Event world.* The vision system has two. One is the world external to our bodies where objects and events occur. The other is the cognitive structures within the mind.
2. *Acquisition.* In the first event world, it happens when light activates the sensors in the retina. In the second it occurs when nerve impulses from the brain are received.
3. *Transmission.* It is achieved by light waves, electric current, or chemical stimuli.
4. *Processing.* Data are stored momentarily in a number of specific sensing mechanisms that detect color, edge contour, and so on.
5. *Utilization.* Processed data are used to recognize objects and actions. Missing data are filled in by making hypotheses about the events, and then testing those assumptions for validity.
6. *Transfer.* Relaying information to the mind's network of cognitive states is how the system affects the event world.

Appendix H
Classifying Information

Information can be sorted into two broad categories. One, facts and opinions, pertains to individual events and actions. The other, theories and processes, is composed of groups of events and actions. Within each division, the credibility of each entry is assessed.

Facts and Opinions

Facts and opinions have three levels of believability. In descending order they are observed phenomena and causal relationships, associative pairings, and opinions or intuitions. Items in the first class occur regularly, such as the events that are studied in the natural sciences. Associative pairings have merely a high probability of occurrence. They are produced by controlled experiments. Often they generate interest in additional studies that reveal the causal relationships suggested in the associations. The least credible class is opinions or intuitions. Their value is directly related to the faith that is placed in the expertise of those expressing their views. Key informant reviews (Straub & Wetherbe, 1989) are opinion surveys that can produce somewhat reliable data.

Theories and Processes

Theories and processes relate bodies of data. Assessing their veracity is difficult, and may be too costly to pursue. But some measures can be taken.

First, it can be determined with some confidence that theories and processes function as described. Logic, mathematics, and common sense can be used to check simple operations. The more complex assemblages need to be exercised. There are many researchers who rely on computers to test their ideas. Theories and processes that can be developed into a working program are more credible than ones that cannot. The ordeal of getting software to run, especially artificial intelligence programs, exposes many inconsistencies and gaps of understanding. Numerous contributions to several fields of study have been made in this way.

Second, the facts used to support a theory can be assessed. Results from controlled experiments are the most believable, provided that they have been properly conducted, are repeatable, and are applicable to the situation (Brooks, 1980; Shneiderman, 1980; Allen, 1982; Sondheimer & Relles, 1982; Brooks et al., 1983). Protocol analysis and cogent observations are less credible. Both are subjective interpretations of events. In the former, the fact that individuals relate the procedures they use while they solve problems raises doubts about its utility. The act of reporting events may alter the sequence and processes that would normally be employed. Interpreting the data is difficult. Is the protocol unique to the individual, or to the situation? Just how broadly can the results be applied? The last question may also be asked of observations. Dijkstra's (1968) admonition against using "GOTO" statements is one example of an overgeneralization. There are cases in which the addition of "GOTO" statements will bring a degree of clarity to a program (see Chapter 13). Another example is the assumption by McCabe (1976) and others (Gill & Kemerer, 1991) that the "IF" statement is a central component of software complexity. "IF" statements can be made easy to understand, and may only be a minor factor in the complexity of a program (see Chapter 13). The least reliable of the material considered are opinion surveys of nonexperts and engineering reports.

The overall criteria for accepting material are based on the assumption that items of information and knowledge collected from different sources and from many perspectives will be generally consistent and tend to confirm one another. Principles and tenets from basic research are expected to hold when applied. Throughout the information and knowledge base many relationships will be established. Each connection will help to validate other components in the system. Items that are anomalous and lack persuasive arguments are discarded.

Appendix I
Naming as a Shortening Process

The naming process is one that reduces the number of symbols employed to represent a referent. Although names may be shortened in different ways, they must remain acceptable to their intended audience. The speaker's "shorthand agreement" addresses some of the criteria for name acceptability (Carroll, 1983). The agreement postulates that a speaker may use a shortened form to represent a category only if it captures the intended context, and is specific, lucid, and discernible to the audience.

John Carroll (1983) has identified four schemes to shorten names. They are category ellipsis, location ellipsis, appellation formation, and explicit metonomy. Category ellipsis is a method that shortens a name by omitting category words, and always produces a true namehead.[8] Utilizing this approach, the name Sports Car Driver of the Year is simplified to Driver of the Year. In similar fashion the second method drops location words. However, it may not generate a true namehead. Appellation formation is a method that does not produce a namehead. The shortened name is created by placing the definite article "the" in front of the product of some reduction scheme. For an abstract pattern such as X category-word Y, the shortened form could be "the" category-word. With this method, Pike Place Market is abbreviated to The Market.

Explicit metonomy is best defined through an illustration. The Pittsburgh Pirates is the name of a baseball franchise. However, within the realm of the major leagues, the club is commonly referred to as simply Pittsburgh.

Shortening names into simpler forms is a process that is also observed in the computer environment (Rich, 1984). In situations where command names are used to interface with the computer, and enough flexibility is given for creating names, computer users will also shorten names. For a new task, they will initially employ English-like command name statements. But as their familiarity with the task increases, their responses correspondingly become more abbreviated. The more they know about their context and the more skilled they become, the fewer symbols they need to express referent meaning.

---

[8] Nameheads are shortened names that retain the function of the name.

Appendix J
Miniature Artificial Languages

A miniature artificial language (MAL) is a set of letter string permutations obtained from a symbol network. Usually the permutations consist of five to ten characters. By observing how people learn MALs, the general strategies for extracting symbol pair association rules can be discovered, and the different conditions under which learning is facilitated be discerned. Understanding the process of rule acquisition provides insights into word recognition and letter position prominence within words (McLaughlin, 1981).

The knowledge gained from MAL research can be used to develop abbreviation schemes that better evoke the name antecedent.

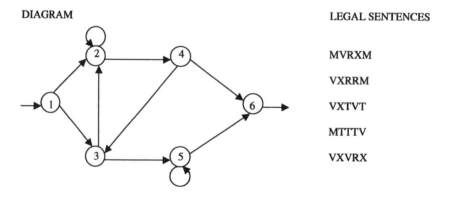

DIAGRAM

LEGAL SENTENCES

MVRXM

VXRRM

VXTVT

MTTTV

VXVRX

Figure 12. Miniature Artificial Language. From "Implicit Learning: An Analysis of the Form and Structure of a Body of Tacit Knowledge" by S. Reber and S. Lewis, 1977, *Cognition*, 5.

Appendix K
Cognitive Grammar

The traditional approach to language study and analysis is to treat it as a separate discipline, apart from the broader issues of cognitive psychology. Unique features of language, such as syntax, semantics, lexicon, and the like, are defined to operate separately. If meaning is addressed it is determined through truth conditions maintained in a formal logic. It is from this tradition that Ronald Langacker's (1986) cognitive grammar departs.

Overview

Cognitive grammar holds that any effort to partition language is arbitrary. The formalisms and divisions, normally a part of language, are absent (Langacker, 1986; Humphreys, Bain, & Pike, 1989). It combines such functions into a continuous operation composed of symbolic units.

Cognitive grammar also departs from the notion of using basic features to represent semantic networks, and of interpreting all meaning through semantic primitives. In it, semantic networks are conceived as taking on the traits of the cognitive domain. The words and names contained therein are structured in a network of interrelated meanings (see Figure 13). The ways they can be used are restricted by the associations they make with other entities. Each association varies in strength and saliency. Over time, they evolve from simple structures to complex hierarchies.

Nodes within the structure are created from operations performed on concepts at lower levels. Each person is endowed with the ability to structure the contents of a domain in multiple ways. Each person's network is also unique. The extent and robustness of networks cannot be precisely ascertained.

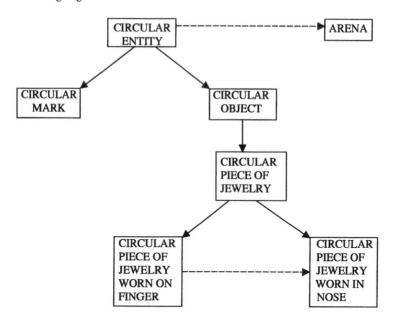

Figure 13. Meaning Network. From "Cognitive Grammar" by R. W. Langacker, 1986, *Cognitive Science*, 10.

Sentence Construction

Cognitive grammar is computational. It builds sentences by combining items from a set of cognitive primitives. Among its operations are a sense of time, operations performed in two- or three-dimensional spaces, domains of senses (e.g., color, temperature, visual coordination, etc.), emotive domains, and so on. The grammar does not make exact distinctions as to what is linguistically relevant. An expression may draw its meaning from one or several domains in the network.

In cognitive grammar expressions are built through a progressive assembly of meaning components. The primary operation projects a "profile" onto a domain or context called a "base." Meaning is derived from the relationship of the profile to the base. Other aspects of a concept, such as granularity, perspective, and background expectations, may also be added.

The relevant saliency of the components in an expression bears a similarity to traditional sentence construction. An elevated item called a "trajector" relates to its "landmarks" in the same fashion that a subject does to its object.

In the grammar, the traditional functions of syntax and semantics are handled as an undifferentiated assortment of symbolic representations. Deep structures, which normally affect meaning, are not posited. Correct usages, or well formedness, are achieved through patterns that define the specific relationships one symbol or structure may have with another. Influencing it are subtle deviations in concept, intended meaning, and the manner in which a person views and partitions the world. From these rules complex expressions are formed.

An example of cognitive grammar is shown in Figure 14, representing the prepositional phrase "above the table." It is composed of a relational and a nominal structure. Meaning is built by associating the landmark of the preposition with the profile of the noun phrase. In this case, the noun phrase "the table" becomes the object of the preposition because it further defines the preposition's landmark.

Cognitive grammar illustrates some of the dynamics of language. It shows how words attach themselves to basic structures, and how these structures interact when words are combined to create phrases.

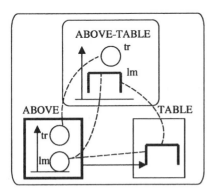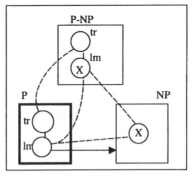

Figure 14. Cognitive Grammar. From "Cognitive Grammar" by R. W. Langacker, 1986, *Cognitive Science*, 10.

Appendix L
Gestalt Psychology

Gestalt psychology interprets our experiences of perception and learning as processes functioning within a system of interrelated conceptual patterns or wholes. Its approach to psychology is diametrically opposed to the connectionist school, based on stimulus-response associations (Hill, 1977). Gestalt psychologists address issues regarding "instructional knowledge," "meaningful apprehension of relationships," and "knowledge which fosters productive reasoning," as contrasted to "rote-memory," "senseless drill," and "reproductive reasoning" (Shneiderman, 1980). The main interest to them is how a conceptual pattern is brought into prominence out of an assemblage of constructions called a perception. Each perception contains a dominant "figure" or gestalt, and a "ground" which is used to refer to other items in the scene (Hill, 1977).

The emphasis on wholes and relationships in gestalt psychology does not preclude a study of the figure's component parts. That may proceed in isolation from their roles within the figure. But to the gestaltist, the primary concern is the meaning that the figure registers with the viewer. For example, with respect to the figure ∴, although one may elect to investigate the dots separately, the chief interest is how the three function together to represent a triangle (Hill, 1977). In gestalt psychology, the properties of the whole are not simply the summation of the features of its component parts (Kanizsa, 1979).

Facts are not studied alone, but as they interrelate with other bodies of information and knowledge to form concepts. Their meanings are dependent on the particular situations in which they occur.[9] When processes interact, their features are reinterpreted, and a new order surfaces and is established. To understand how meaningful learning is attained, the gestaltist investigates the changes that occur among the internal relationships that are brought about as a context is altered (Henle, 1987).

Gestalt psychologists have discovered conditions under which elemental stimuli conceptually combine to appear as a perceptual whole. Six laws govern the formation of visual units. These may also be applied to cognitive processing in general (Katz, 1950; Hill, 1977).

---

[9] Refer also to the discussion on naming in Chapter 5 and on word meaning in Chapter 6.

1. *The law of proximity.* In the absence of interfering conditions, elements will tend to form groups based on their nearness to one another (Katz, 1950; Hill, 1977).

2. *The law of similarity.* When more than one element is viewed, those that are similar will tend to be perceived as a group (Katz, 1950).

3. *The law of closure.* A surface that is enclosed will tend to be perceived as a unit (Katz, 1950; Hill, 1977).

4. *The law of "good" contour, or common destiny.* Within a picture or frame of reference, figure parts that appear to extend or continue to and from each other, tend to be perceived as a unit. This law helps to explain why objects that are brought into contact with one another are viewed as distinct wholes (Katz, 1950).

5. *The law of common movement.* Elements that are moved as a unit are perceived as a whole (Katz, 1950).

6. *The law of experience.* Symbolic forms are understood in part from the context in which they were learned (Katz, 1950).

These laws identify conditions through which a group of elements will become viewed as a unit, but say little about how the unit will be conceptually organized or shaped. That phenomenon is explained by the law of pregnance, which states that a perceptual unit will be interpreted as the simplest form or structure that is permitted under the forces acting upon it. If those conditions are unconstraining, the unit will be seen as having a regular or symmetrical shape. When the medium increases in complexity, the interpretation of the unit becomes more difficult to predict (Koffka, 1935). For example, if a ring containing a small gap in its circumference is scanned quickly, it will be seen as an unbroken circle. The visual sampling did not gather enough data to force a more detailed interpretation containing the gap. The most familiar and meaningful structure that fits into the perceived context is the one that is chosen.

Bibliography

Abran, A., & Nguyenkim, H. (1991). Analysis of maintenance work categories through measurements. *Proceedings of the 1991 Conference on Software Maintenance*, IEEE Computer Society Press, Los Alamitos, Calif., 104–113.

Adams, M. (1979). Models of word recognition. *Cognitive Psychology*, 11, 133–176.

Adelson, B. (1981). Problem solving and the development of abstract categories in programming languages. *Memory & Cognition*, 9(4), 422–433.

Adelson, B., & Soloway, E. (1984). Methodology revisited: The cognitive underpinnings of programmer's behavior. In Salvendy, G., Ed., *Human-Computer Interaction*, Elsevier Science Publishers B.V., Amsterdam.

Adrion, W., Branstad, M., & Cherniavsky, J. (1982). Validation, verification, and testing of computer software. *ACM Computing Surveys*, 14(2), 159–192.

Allen, R. (1982). Cognitive factors in human interaction with computers. *Behaviour and Information Technology*, 1(3), 257–278.

Allen, R., & Reber, A. (1980). Very long term memory for tacit knowledge. *Cognition*, 8, 175–185.

Andrews, S. (1989). Frequency and neighborhood effects on lexical access: Activation or search? *Journal of Experimental Psychology*, 15(5), 802–814.

Arthur, J., Nance, R., & Balci, O. (1993). Establishing software development process control: Technical objectives, operating requirements, and the foundational framework. *Journal of Systems and Software*, 22(2), 117–128.

Arthur, L. (1988). *Software Evolution: The Software Maintenance Challenge*, John Wiley Sons, New York.

Babcock, C. (1987). Staffers seek bolstered image. *Computerworld*, 21(20), 8.

Baecker, R., & Marcus, A. (1986). Design principles for the enhanced presentation of computer source text. *Proceedings of CHI' 86*, ACM, New York.

Bailin, S. (1989). An object-oriented requirements specification method. *Communications of the ACM*, 32(5), 608–623.

Banker, R., Datar, S., Kemerer, C., & Zweig, D. (1993). Software complexity and maintenance costs. *Communications of the ACM*, 36(11), 81–94.

Barnard, P., Hammond, N., MacLean, A., & Morton, J. (1981). Learning and remembering interactive commands. *Proceedings of the ACM Computer Science Conference*, ACM, New York.

Basili, V., & Mills, H. (1982). Understanding and documenting programs. *IEEE Transactions on Software Engineering*, 8(3), 270–283.

Bateson, A., Alexander, R., & Murphy, M. (1987). Cognitive processing differences between novice and expert computer programmers. *International Journal of Man-Machine Studies*, 26, 649–660.

Begg, I., & Green, C. (1988). Repetition and trace interaction: Superadditivity. *Memory & Cognition*, 16(3), 232–242.

Begg, I., Snider, A., Foley, F., & Goddard, R. (1989). The generation effect is no artifact: Generating makes words distinctive. *Journal of Experimental Psychology*, 15(5), 977–989.

Bellezza, F., & Young, D. (1989). Chunking of repeated events in memory. *Journal of Experimental Psychology: Learning, Memory, and Cognition*, 15(5), 990–997.

Benbasat, I., & Wand, Y. (1984). Command abbreviation behavior in human-computer interaction. *Communications of the ACM*, 27(4), 376–382.

Benbasat, I., Dexter, A., & Masulis, P. (1981). An experimental study of the human/computer interface. *Communications of the ACM*, 24(11), 752–762.

Bennett, K. (1991). Automated support of software maintenance. *Information and Software Technology*, 33(1), 74–85.

Berns, G. (1984). Assessing software maintainability. *Communications of the ACM*, 27(1), 14–23.

Black, J., & Moran, T. (1981). Learning and remembering command names. *Proceedings of the ACM Computer Science Conference*, ACM, New York.

Black, J., & Sebrechts, M. (1981). An invited article facilitating human-computer communications. *Applied Psychology*, 2, 149–177.

Boillot, M. (1978). *Understanding FORTRAN*, West Publishing Co., St. Paul, Minn.

Bowen, J., Breuer, P., & Lano, K. (1993). A compendium of formal techniques for software maintenance. *Software Engineering Journal*, 8(5), 253–262.

Bower, G. (1970). Organizational factors in memory. *Cognitive Psychology*, 1, 18–46.

Brooks, F. (1987). No silver bullet: Essence and accidents of software engineering. *Computer*, 20(4), 10–19.

Brooks, R. (1976). How a programmer understands a program: A model. *Technical Report #97*, Department of Information and Computer Science, University of California-Irvine, Irvine, Calif.

Brooks, R. (1980). Studying programmer behavior experimentally: The problems of proper methodology. *Communications of the ACM*, 23(4), 207–213.

Brooks, R. (1981). A theoretical analysis of the role of documentation in the comprehension of computer programs. *Proceedings of the ACM Computer Science Conference*, ACM, New York.

Brooks, R., Black, J., Curtis, B., Ehrlich, K., Ramsey, H., & Soloway, E. (1983). Software psychology: The need for an interdisciplinary program. *NSF/OIR-83007*.

Buschke, H. (1976). Learning is organized by chunking. *Journal of Verbal Learning and Verbal Behavior*, 15, 313–324.

Carroll, J. (1980a). "Purpose" in a cognitive theory of reference. *Bulletin of the Psychonomic Society*, 16(1), 37–40.

Carroll, J. (1980b). The role of context in creating names. *Discourse Processes*, 3, 1–24.

Carroll, J. (1980c). Naming and describing in social communications. *Language and Speech*, 23(4), 309–322.

Carroll, J. (1980d). Naming as a mapping between n-dimensional geometries. *IBM Research Report*, RC-8596.

Carroll, J. (1981). Creating names for things. *Journal of Psycholinguistic Research*, 10(4), 441–455.

Carroll, J. (1982). Creative names for personal files in an interactive computing environment. *International Journal of Man-Machine Studies*, 16, 405–438.

Carroll, J. (1983). Nameheads. *Cognitive Science*, 7, 121–153.

Chambers, F. (1983). Readability formulae and the structure of text. *Education Review*, 5(1), 3–13.

Chambers, S. (1979). Letter and order information in lexical access. *Journal of Verbal Learning and Verbal Behavior*, 18, 225–241.

Chapin, N. (1986). Veil of obscurity masks need for maintenance training. *Computerworld*, 20(17), 59.

Charles, W., & Miller, G. (1989). Contexts of antonymous adjectives. *Applied Linguistics*, 10, 357–375.

Chase, W., & Simon, H. (1973). Perception in chess. *Cognitive Psychology*, 4, 55–81.

Chaudhary, B., & Sahasrabuddhe, H. (1985). A study in dimensions of psychological complexity of programs. *International Journal of Man-Machine Studies*, 23, 113–133.

Chechile, R., Fleischman, R., & Sadoski, D. (1986). The effects of syntactic complexity on the human-computer interaction. *Human Factors*, 28(11), 11–22.

Chen, T. (1978). Program complexity and programming productivity. *IEEE Transactions on Software Engineering*, SE-4(3), 187–194.

Cherry, J. (1986). An experimental evaluation of prefix and postfix notation in command language syntax. *International Journal of Man-Machine Studies*, 24, 365–374.

Chomsky, N. (1972). *Studies on Semantics in Generative Grammar*. Mouton, The Hague.

Chudleigh, M. (1990). Software and safety: How compatible are they? *Information and Software Technology*, 32(5), 323–329.

Cole, J. (1978). *ANSI FORTRAN IV: A Structured Program Approach*, William C. Brown Company Publishers, Dubuque, Iowa.

Collofello, J., & Gosalia, B. (1993). An application of causal analysis to the software modification process. *Software-Practice and Experience*, 23(10), 1095–1105.

Corkill, A., Bruning, R., & Glover, J. (1988). Advance organizers: Concrete versus abstract. *Journal of Education Research*, 82(2), 76–81.

Couger, J., & Shannon, L. (1976). *FORTRAN IV: A P. I. Approach Including Structured Programming*, Richard D. Irwin, Inc., Homewood, Ill.

Coulter, N. (1983). Software science and cognitive psychology, *IEEE Transactions on Software Engineering*, 9(2), 166–171.

Coward, P. (1991). Symbol execution and testing. *Information and Software Technology*, 33(1), 53–64.

Curtis, B. (1981). A review of human factors research on programming languages and specifications. *Proceedings of the ACM Computer Science Conference*, ACM, New York.

Curtis, B., Forman, I., Brooks, R., Soloway, E., & Ehrlich, K. (1984). Psychological perspectives for software science. *Information Processing & Management*, 20(1,2), 81–96.

Curtis, B., Sheppard, S., Kruesi-Bailey, E., Bailey, J., & Boehm-Davis, D. (1989). Experimental evaluation of software documentation formats. *The Journal of Systems and Software*, 9, 167–207.

Davis, J. (1984). Chunks: A basis for complexity measurement. *Information Processing & Management*, 20(1,2), 119–127.

Debons, A., Horne, E., & Cronenweth, S. (1988). *Information Science: An Integrated View*, G. K. Hall & Co., Boston.

Debons, A., King, D., Mansfield, U., & Shirey, D. (1981). *The Information Professional: Survey of an Emerging Field*, Marcel Dekker, Inc., New York.

den Heyer, K. (1985). On the nature of the proportion effect in semantic priming. *Acta Psychologica*, 60, 25–38.

DeYoung, G., Kampen, G., & Topolski, J. (1981). Analyzer-generated and human-judged predictors of computer program readability. *Proceedings of the ACM Computer Science Conference*, ACM, New York.

Dijkstra, E. (1968). GOTO statement considered harmful (Letter). *Communications of the ACM*, 11(3), 147–148.

Dirlam, D. (1972). Most efficient chunk sizes. *Cognitive Psychology*, 3, 355–359.

Dock, V. (1979). *Structured FORTRAN Programming*, West Publishing Company, St. Paul, Minn.

Dowty, D. (1979). *Word Meaning and Montague Grammar: The Semantics of Verbs and Times in Generative Semantics and in Montague's PTQ*, D. Reidel Publishing Company, Dordrecht, Holland.

Duchek, J., & Neely, J. (1989). A dissociative word-frequency X levels-of-processing interaction in episodic recognition and lexical decision tasks. *Memory & Cognition*, 17(2), 148–162.

Duffy, S., Henderson, J., & Morris, R. (1989). Semantic facilitation of lexical access during sentence processing. *Journal of Experimental Psychology*, 15(5), 791–801.

Duncan, M. (1989). Give maintenance some respect in training too, upkeep of systems remains the Rodney Dangerfield of IS. *Computerworld*, 23(47), 132–133.

Dyer, M., & Kouchakdjian, A. (1990). Correctness verification: Alternative to structural software testing. *Information and Software Technology*, 32(1). 53–59.

Eason, K., & Damodaran, L. (1981). The needs of the commercial user. In Coombs, M., & Alty, J., Eds., *Computing Skills and the User Interface*, Academic Press. New York.

Edelstein, D. (1993). Report on the IEEE STD 1219-1993-standard for software maintenance. *ACM SIGSOFT Software Engineering Notes*, 18(4), 94–95.

Eerkes, G. (1991). Profiling computer science master's programs. *Communications of the ACM*, 34(1), 100–109.

Ehrenreich, S. (1985). Computer abbreviations: Evidence and synthesis. *Human Factors*, 27(2), 143–155.

Elmer-Dewitt, P. (1990). Ghost in the machine. *Time*, 135(5), 58–59.

Elshoff, J., & Marcotty, M. (1982). Improving program readability to aid modification. *Communications of the ACM*, 25(8), 522–526.

Fisher, D. (1983). Global variables versus local variables. *Software-Practice and Experience*, 13, 467–469.

Fitzsimmons, A., & Love, T. (1978). A review and evaluation of software science. *ACM Computer Surveys*, 10(1), 3–18.

Flynn, R. (1987). *An Introduction to Information Science*, Marcel Dekker, Inc., New York.

Forester, T., & Morrison, P. (1990). Computer unreliability and social vulnerability. *Future*, 22(5), 463–474.

Fried, L. (1982). Nine principles for ergonomic software. *Datamation*, 28(12), 164–166.

Friedman, F., & Koffman, E. (1981). *Problem Solving and Structured Programming in FORTRAN*, Addison-Wesley Publishing Company, Reading, Mass.

Gabriele, E., & Frauenhofer, M. (1984). Abbreviations: A challenge to medical information. *Journal of Clinical Computing*, 12(5), 140–154.

Gannon, J. (1976). An experiment for the evaluation of language features. *International Journal of Man-Machine Studies*, 8, 61–73.

Gardiner, J., Gregg, V., & Hampton, J. (1988). Word frequency and generation effects. *Journal of Experimental Psychology*, 14(4), 687–693.

Gibson, V., & Senn, J. (1989). System structure and software maintenance performance. *Communications of the ACM*, 32(3), 347–358.

Gill, A. (1962). *Introduction to the Theory of Finite-State Machines*, McGraw-Hill, Inc., New York.

Gill, G., & Kemerer, C. (1991). Cyclomatic complexity density and software maintenance productivity. *IEEE Transactions on Software Engineering*, 17(12), 1284–1288.

Glass, R. (1979). *Software Reliability Guidebook*, Prentice-Hall, Inc., Englewood Cliffs, N. J.

Glass, R. (1982). *Modern Programming Practices: A Report From Industry*, Prentice-Hall, Inc., Englewood Cliffs, N. J.

Glass, R., & Noiseux, R. (1981). *Software Maintenance Guidebook*, Prentice-Hall, Inc., Englewood Cliffs, N. J.

Gorla, N. (1991). Techniques for application software maintenance. *Information and Software Technology*, 33(1), 65–73.

Gould, J. (1975). Some psychological evidence on how people debug computer programs. *International Journal of Man-Machine Studies*, 7, 151–182.

Gould, J., & Drongowski, P. (1974). An exploratory study of computer program debugging. *Human Factors*, 16, 258–277.

Gregory, R. (1990). *Eye and Brain: The Psychology of Seeing*, Princeton University Press, Princeton, N. J.

Gremillion, L. (1984). Determinants of program repair maintenance requirements. *Communications of the ACM*, 27(8), 826–832.

Grochow, J. (1993). Tidal wave approaching. *Computerworld*, 27(38), 41.

Gross, D., Fischer, U., & Miller, G. (1989). The organization of adjectival meaning. *Journal of Memory and Language*, 28, 92–106.

Grudin, J., & Barnard, P. (1984). The cognitive demands of learning and representing command names for text editing. *Human Factors*, 26(4), 407–422.

Grusser, O., & Grusser-Cornehls, U. (1986). Physiology of vision. In Schmidt, R., Ed., *Fundamentals of Sensory Physiology*, Springer-Verlag, Berlin, Germany.

GSA-General Services Administration (1981). *Software Improvement—A Needed Process in the Federal Government*, Report Number OSD-81-102, Falls Church, Va.

GSA-General Services Administration (1983a). *Software Improvement Process—Its Phases and Tasks*, Report Number OSD/FCSC-83/006, Falls Church, Va.

GSA-General Services Administration (1983b). *Guidelines for Planning and Implementing a Software Improvement Program (SIP)*, Report Number OSD/FCSC-83/004, Falls Church, Va.

Guimaraes, T. (1983). Managing application program maintenance expenditures. *Communications of the ACM*, 26(10), 739–746.

Halstead, M. (1979). Guest editorial on software science. *IEEE Transactions on Software Engineering*, SE-5(2), 74–75.

Hamlet, D., & Taylor, R. (1990). Partition testing does not inspire confidence. *IEEE 206 Transactions on Software Engineering*, 16(12). 1402–1411.

Hayakawa, S. (1941). *Language in Thought and Action*, Harcourt, Brace and Company, New York.

Henle, M. (1987). Koffka's principles after fifty years. *Journal of the History of the Behavioral Sciences*, 23(1), 14–21.

Hill, L., Jr., (1981). *Structured Programming in FORTRAN*, Prentice-Hall, Inc., Englewood Cliffs, N. J.

Hill, W. (1977). *Learning: A Survey of Psychological Interpretations*, Harper & Row, Publishers, New York.

Hirsh-Pasek, K., Nudelman, S., & Schneider, M. (1982). An experimental evaluation of abbreviation schemes in limited lexicons. *Behaviour & Information Technology*, (4), 327–346.

Hodge, M., & Pennington, F. (1973). Some studies of word abbreviation behavior. *Journal of Experimental Psychology*, 98(2), 350–361.

Horton, K. (1989). The processing of spatially transformed text. *Memory & Cognition*, 17(3), 283–291.

Howden, W. (1982). Validation of scientific programs. *ACM Computing Surveys*, 14(2), 193–227.

Humphreys, G. (1987). Objects, words, brains and computers: Framing the correspondence problem in object and word recognition. *Bulletin of the British Psychological Society*, 40, 207–210.

Humphreys, M., Bain, J., & Pike, R. (1989). Different ways to cue a coherent memory system: A theory for episodic, semantic, and procedural tasks. *Psychological Review*, 96(2), 208–233.

Irons, D. (1981). Cognitive correlates of programming task in novice programmers. *Proceedings of the ACM Computer Science Conference*, ACM, New York.

Isner, J. (1982). A FORTRAN programming methodology based on data abstractions. *Communications of the ACM*, 25(10), 686–696.

Jacky, J., & Kalet, I. (1987). An object-oriented programming discipline for standard PASCAL. *Communications of the ACM*, 30(9), 772–776.

James, E. (1981). The user interface: How we may compute. In Coombs, M. & Alty, J., Eds., *Computing Skills and the User Interface*, Academic Press, New York.

Jeng, B., & Weyuker, E. (1989). Some observations on partition testing. *ACM SIGSOFT: Software Engineering Notes*, 14(1), 131–140.

Johns, E., & Swanson, L, (1988). The generation effect with nonwords. *Journal of Experimental Psychology*, 14(1), 180–190.

Kaiser, G. (1988). Marvel: Intelligence assistance for software development and maintenance (Colloquium). Seattle, Wa.: University of Washington, Department of Computer Science.

Kanizsa, G. (1979). *Organization in Vision: Essays on Gestalt Perception*, Praeger Publishers, Praeger Special Studies, New York.

Kassin, S., & Reber, A. (1979). Locus of control and the learning of an artificial language. *Journal of Research in Personality*, 13, 112–118.

Katz, D. (1950). *Gestalt Psychology: Its Nature and Significance*, The Ronald Press Company, New York.

Kelly, M., & Chapanis, A. (1977). Limited vocabulary natural language dialogue. *International Journal of Man-Machine Studies*, 9, 479–501.

Kernigham, B., & Plauger, P. (1978). *The Elements of Programming Style*, McGraw-Hill Book Company, New York.

Klapp, S. (1987). Short-term memory limits in human performance. In Hancock, P., Ed., *Human Factors Psychology*, Elsevier Science Publishers B.V., Amsterdam.

Klapp, S., & Netick, A. (1988). Multiple resources for processing and storage in short-term working memory. *Human Factors*, 30(5), 617–632.

Kochen, M. (1984). Coding for recording and recall of information. *Information Processing & Management*, 20(3), 343–354.

Koffka, K. (1935). *Principles of Gestalt Psychology*, Harcourt, Brace and Company, New York.

Koriat, A., & Melkman, R. (1987). Depth of processing and memory organization. *Psychological Research*, 49, 173–181.

Korson, T., & McGregor, J. (1990). Understanding object-oriented: A unifying paradigm. *Communications of the ACM*, 33(9), 40–60.

Kotovsky, K., & Simon, H. (1990). What makes some problems really hard: Explorations in the problem space of difficulty. *Cognitive Psychology*, 22, 143–183.

Kotovsky, K., Hayes, J., & Simon, H. (1985). Why are some problems hard?: Evidence from tower of Hanoi. *Cognitive Psychology*, 17, 248–294.

Krug, D., George, B., Hannon, S., & Glover, J. (1989). The effect of outlines and headings on readers' recall of text. *Contemporary Educational Psychology*, 14, 111–123.

Landauer, T., Galotti, K., & Hartwell, S. (1983). Natural command names and initial learning: A study of text-editing terms. *Communications of the ACM*, 26(7), 495–503.

Langacker, R. (1986). An introduction to cognitive grammar. *Cognitive Science*, 10, 1–40.

Laprie, J. (1990). On the assessment of safety-critical software systems. *12th International Conference on Software Engineering*, IEEE Computer Society Press, Los Alamitos, Calif.

Leveson, N. (1986). Software safety: Why, what, and how. *ACM Computing Surveys*, 18(2), 125–163.

Leveson, N. (1990). Evaluation of software safety. *12th International Conference on Software Engineering*, IEEE Society Press, Los Alamitos, Calif.

Leveson, N. (1991). Software safety in embedded computer systems. *Communications of the ACM*, 34(2), 34–46.

Lewis, P. (1980). Information systems is an engineering discipline (Letter). *Communications of the ACM*, 32(9), 1045–1047.

Lientz, B. (1980). *Software Maintenance Management*, Addison-Wesley Publishing Company, Inc., Reading, Mass.

Lientz, B. (1983). Issues in software maintenance. *ACM Computing Surveys*, 15(3), 271–278.

Lientz, B., & Swanson, E. (1981). Problems in application software maintenance. *Communications of the ACM*, 24(11), 763–769.

Linger, R., Mills, H., & Witt, B. (1979). *Structured Programming: Theory and Practice*, Addison-Wesley Publishing Company, Inc., Reading, Mass.

MacLeod, C. (1989). Word context during initial exposure influences degree of priming in word fragment completion. *Journal of Experimental Psychology: Learning, Memory, and Cognition*, 15(3), 398–406.

Magel, K., Austing, R., Berztiss, A., Engel, G., Hamblen, J., Hoffman, A., & Mathis, R. (1981). Recommendations for master's level programs in computer science. *Communications of the ACM*, 24(3), 115–123.

Mannes, W., & Kintsch, W. (1987). Knowledge organizations and text organization. *Cognition and Instruction*, 4(2), 91–115.

Marcus, A. (1981). Typographic design for interfaces. *Proceedings of the ACM Computer Science Conference*, ACM, New York.

Marick, B. (1990). A survey of test effectiveness and cost studies. Department of Computer Science, University of Illinois, Urbana, Ill.

Marohn, K., & Hochhaus, L. (1988). Semantic priming increases and repetition priming decreases apparent stimulus duration. *The Journal of General Psychology*, 115(1), 51–61.

Martin, J., & McClure, C. (1983). *Software Maintenance: The Problem and its Solution*, Prentice-Hall, Inc., Englewood Cliffs, N. J.

Masson, M. (1988). The interaction of sentence context and perceptual analysis in word identification. *Memory & Cognition*, 16(6), 489–496.

Mayer, R. (1981). How novices learn computer programming. *ACM Computing Surveys*, 13(1), 121–141.

McCabe, T. (1976). A complexity measure, *IEEE Transactions on Software Engineering*, SE-2(4), 308–320.

McClure, C. (1981). *Managing Software Development and Maintenance*, Van Nostrand Reinhold Company, New York.

McKeithen, K., Reitman, J., Rueter, H., & Hirtle, S. (1981). Knowledge organization and skill differences in computer programmers. *Cognitive Psychology*, 13, 307–325.

McLaughlin, B. (1981). On the use of miniature artificial languages in second-language research. *Applied Psycholinguistics*, 1(4), 357–369.

Miller, G. (1956). The magical number seven, plus or minus two: Some limits on our capacity for processing information. *The Psychological Review*, 63(2), 81–97.

Miller, G., & Charles, W. (1991). Contextual correlates of semantic similarity. *Language and Cognitive Processes*, 6(1), 1–28.

Miller, G., & Johnson-Laird, P. (1976). *Language and Perception*, The Belknap Press of Harvard University Press, Cambridge, Mass.

Miller, L. (1974). Programming by non-programmers. *International Journal of Man-Machine Studies*, 6, 237–260.

Miller, L. (1981). Natural language programming: Styles, strategies, and contrasts. *IBM Systems Journal*, 20(2), 184–215.

Mitchell, D. (1989). How many memory systems?: Evidence from aging. *Journal of Experimental Psychology: Learning, Memory, and Cognition*, 15(1), 31–49.

Moher, T., & Schneider, G. (1982). Methodology and experimental research in software engineering. *International Journal of Man-Machine Studies*, 16, 65–87.

Moret, B. (1982). Decision trees and diagrams. *ACM Computing Surveys*, 14(4), 593–623.

Mullin, P., & Egeth, H. (1989). Capacity limitations in visual word processing. *Journal of Experimental Psychology*, 15(1), 111–123.

Mutter, S., & Hashtroudi, S. (1987). Cognitive effort and the word frequency effect in recognition and lexical decision. *American Journal of Psychology*, 100(1), 93–116.

Mynatt, B. (1984). The effect of semantic complexity on the comprehension of program modules. *International Journal of Man-Machine Studies*, 21, 91–103.

Nagata, H. (1976). Quantitative and qualitative analysis of experience in acquisition of a miniature artificial language. *Japanese Psychological Research*, 18(4), 174–182.

Nelson, D., Bajo, M., McEvoy, C., & Schreiber, T. (1989). Prior knowledge: The effects of natural category size on memory for implicitly encoded concepts. *Journal of Experimental Psychology*, 15(5), 957–967.

Nelson, D., Keelean, P., & Negrao, M. (1989). Word-fragment cueing: The lexical search hypothesis. *Journal of Experimental Psychology*, 15(3), 388–397.

Neumann, P. (1991). Inside risks: Certifying professionals. *Communications of the ACM*, 34(2), 130.

Newell, A., & Simon, H. (1972). *Human Problem Solving*, Prentice-Hall, Inc., Englewood Cliffs, N. J.

Newsome, S., & Katz, I. (1987). The influence of structure on computer program comprehension. *Behavior Research Methods. Instruments, & Computers*, 19(2), 152–155.

Nickerson, R. (1969). Man-computer interaction: A challenge for human factors research. *Ergonomics*, 12(4), 164–180.

Nilsson, N. (1980). *Principles of Artificial Intelligence*, Tioga Publishing Company, Palo Alto, Calif.

Norcio, A. (1981). Indentation, documentation and programmer comprehension. *Proceedings of the ACM Computer Science Conference*, ACM, New York.

Norcio, A., & Kerst, S. (1983). Human memory organization for computer programs. *Journal of the American Society for Information Science*, 34(2), 109–114.

Norman, D., & Bobrow, D. (1975). On data-limited and resource-limited processes. *Cognitive Psychology*, 7, 44–64.

Olson, D. (1970). Language and thought: Aspects of a cognitive theory of semantics. *Psychological Review*, 77(4), 257–273.

Omar, A., & Mohammed, F. (1991). A survey of software functional testing methods. *ACM SIGSOFT Software Engineering Notes*, 16(2), 75–82.

Ould, M., & Unwin, C. (1986). *Testing in Software Development*, The Press Syndicate of the University of Cambridge.

Palermo, D., & Parrish, M. (1971). Rule acquisition as a function of number and frequency of exemplar presentation. *Journal of Verbal Learning and Verbal Behavior*, 10, 44–51.

Palmer, J., & Jonides, J. (1988). Automatic memory search and the effects of information load and irrelevant information. *Journal of Experimental Psychology*, 14(1), 136–144.

Parnas, D., van Schouwen, J., & Kwan, S. (1990). Evaluation of safety-critical software. *Communications of the ACM*, 33(6), 636–648.

Pennington, N. (1987). Stimulus structures and mental representations in expert comprehension of computer programs. *Cognitive Psychology*, 19, 295–341.

Perlman, G. (1984). Natural artificial languages: Low level processes. *International Journal of Man-Machine Studies*, 20, 373–419.

Peterson, J. (1977). Petri nets. *ACM Computing Surveys*, 9(3), 223–252.

Pezdek, K., Whetstone, T., Reynolds, K., Askari, N., & Dougherty, T. (1989). Memory for real-world scenes: The role of consistency with schema expectation. *Journal of Experimental Psychology: Learning, Memory, and Cognition*, 15(4), 587–595.

Pickard, M., & Carter, B. (1993). Maintainability: What is it and how do we measure it?, *ACM SIGSOFT Software Engineering Notes*, 18(3), 136–139.

Pinto, J., & Soloway, E. (1988). Providing the requisite knowledge via software documentation. *Proceedings of CHI' 88*, ACM, New York.

Polya, G. (1957). *How to Solve It*, Doubleday and Company, Inc., Garden City, N. Y.

Pylyshyn, Z. (1984). *Computation and Cognition*, The MIT Press, Cambridge, Mass.

Ranney, M. (1987). The role of structure context in perception: Syntax in the recognition of algebraic expressions. *Memory & Cognition*, 15(1), 29–41.

Ratcliff, R., & McKoon, R. (1988). A retrieval theory of priming in memory. *Psychological Review*, 95(3), 385–408.

Reber, A. (1969). Transfer of syntactic structure in synthetic languages. *Journal of Experimental Psychology*, 81, 115–119.

Reber, A., & Allen, R. (1978). Analogic and abstraction strategies in synthetic grammar learning: A functionalist interpretation. *Cognition*, 6, 189–221.

Reber, A., & Lewis, S. (1977). Implicit learning: An analysis of the form and structure of a body of tacit knowledge. *Cognition*, 5, 333–361.

Reber, A., Allen, R., & Regan, S. (1985). Syntactical learning and judgment, still unconscious and still abstract: Comment on Dulany, Carlson, and Dewey. *Journal of Experimental Psychology: General*, 114(1), 17–24.

Reber, A., Kassin, S., Lewis, S., & Cantor, G. (1980). On the relationship between implicit and explicit modes in the learning of a complex rule structure. *Journal of Experimental Psychology: Human Learning and Memory*, 6(5), 492–502.

Reisner, P. (1977). Use of psychological experimentation as an aid to development of a query language. *IEEE Transactions on Software Engineering*, 3(3), 218–229.

Reisner, P. (1981). Formal grammar and human factors design of an interactive graphics system. *IEEE Transactions on Software Engineering*, SE-7(2), 229–240.

Rich, E. (1984). Natural-language interfaces. *Computer*, 17(9), 39–47.

Richards, D. (1988). Dynamic concepts and functionality: The influence of multiple representations and environmental constraints on categorization. *Human Development*, 31, 11–19.

Richards, L., & Heller, F. (1976). Recognition thresholds as a function of word length. *American Journal of Psychology*, 89(3), 455–466.

Robson, D., Bennett, K., Cornelius, B., & Munro, M. (1991). Approaches to program comprehension. *Journal of Systems and Software*, 14(2), 79–84.

Rogers, W., & Moeller, G. (1984). Comparison of abbreviation methods: Measures of preference and decoding performance. *Human Factors*, 26(1), 49–59.

Rombach, H. (1991). Software reuse: A key to the maintenance problem. *Information and Software Technology*, 33(1), 86–92.

Rosenberg, J. (1981). Evaluating the suggestiveness of command names. *Proceedings of the ACM Computer Science Conference*, ACM, New York.

Rosenberg, J. (1983). A feature approach to command names. *Proceedings CHI'83 Human Factors in Computing Systems*, ACM, New York.

Rosenberg, S. (1987). Semantic integration in sentence memory. *American Journal of Psychology*, 100(2), 253–266.

Russell, G. (1991). Experience with inspection in ultralarge-scale developments. *IEEE Software*, 25–31.

Ryge, S. (1981). Evaluating structured COBOL as a software engineering discipline. *Data Base*, 12(3), 3–6.

Saariluoma, P., & Sajaniema, J. (1989). Visual information chunking in spreadsheet calculation. *International Journal of Man-Machine Studies*, 30(4/5), 474–488.

Scapin, S. (1981). Computer commands labelled by users versus imposed commands and the effect of structuring rules on recall. *Proceedings of the ACM Computer Science Conference*, ACM, New York.

Schank, R. (1980). Language and memory. *Cognitive Science*, 4, 243–284.

Schneider, W., & Detweiler, M. (1987). A connectionist/control architecture for working memory. In Bower, G., Ed., *The Psychology of Learning and Motivation*, 21, Academic Press, New York.

Schwanenflugel, P., & Stowe, R. (1989). Context availability and the processing of abstract and concrete words in sentences. *Reading Research Quarterly*, 24(1), 114–125.

Shannon, C., & Weaver, W. (1949). *The Mathematical Theory of Communication*, University of Illinois Press, Urbana, Ill.

Sheil, B. (1981). The psychological study of programming. *ACM Computing Surveys*, 13(1), 101–120.

Sheppard, S., Curtis, B., Milliman, P., & Love, T. (1979). Modern coding practices and programmer performance. *Computer*, 12(12), 41–49.

Sheppard, S., Kruesi, E., & Bailey, J. (1984). An empirical evaluation of software documentation formats. In Thomas, J., & Schneider, M., Eds., *Human Factors and Computer Systems*, Ablex Publishing Corporation, Norwood, N. J.

Shneiderman, B. (1976). Exploratory experiments in programming behavior. *International Journal of Computer and Information Science*, 592), 123–143.

Shneiderman, B. (1980). *Software Psychology: Human Factors in Computer and Information Systems*, Winthrop, New York.

Sime, M., Arblaster, A., & Green, T. (1977). Reducing programming errors in nested conditionals by prescribing a writing procedure. *International Journal of Man-Machine Studies*, 9, 119–126.

Sime, M., Green, T., & Guest, D. (1973). Psychological evaluation of two conditional constructions used in computer languages. *International Journal of Man-Machine Studies*, 5, 105–113.

Simon, H. (1969). *The Sciences of the Artificial*, The MIT Press, Cambridge, Mass.

Simon, H. (1986). The information processing explanation of gestalt phenomena. *Computers in Human Behavior*, 2, 241–255.

Simon, H. (1990). Invariants of human behavior. In Rosenzweig, M., & Porter, L., Eds., *Annual Review of Psychology*, 41.

Singer, M., Parbery, G., & Jakobson, L. (1988). Focused search of semantic cases in question answering. *Memory & Cognition*, 16(2), 146–157.

Smith, D. (1975). Edit for tonsils and adenoids data (Computer Program). Pittsburgh, Pa.: University of Pittsburgh, School of Medicine, Department of Community Medicine.

Smith, D. (1981). Engine fuel flow (Computer Program). Seattle, Wa.: Boeing Commercial Airplane Company Support Division, Flight Test Computing.

Soloway, E. (1984). A cognitively-based methodology for designing languages/environments/methodologies. *Proceedings of the ACM SIGSOFT/SIGPLAN Software Engineering Symposium on Practical Software Development*, ACM, New York.

Sondheimer, N., & Relles, N. (1982). Human factors and user assistance in interactive computing systems: An introduction. *IEEE Transactions on Systems, Man, and Cybernetics*, 12(2), 102–107.

Spencer, H. (1968). *The Visible Word*, Hasting House Publishers, New York.

Straub, D., & Wetherbe, J. (1989). Information technologies for the 1990s: An organizational impact perspective. *Communications of the ACM*, 32(11), 1328–1339.

Streeter, L., Ackroff, J., & Taylor, G. (1983). On abbreviating command names. *The Bell System Technical Journal*, 62(6), 1807–1826.

Stroud, J. (1955). The fine structure of psychological time. In Quastler, H., Ed., *Information Theory in Psychology*, The Free Press.

Taft, M., & Forster, K. (1976). Lexical storage and retrieval of polymorphemic and polysyllabic words. *Journal of Verbal Learning and Verbal Behavior*, 15, 607–620.

Thomas, M. (1990). Assessing failure probabilities in safety-critical systems containing software. *12th International Conference on Software Engineering*, IEEE Computer Society Press, Los Alamitos, Calif.

Tulving, E. (1985). How many memory systems are there? *American Psychologist*, 40(4), 385–398.

Tulving, E. (1993). What is episodic memory? *Current Directions in Psychological Science*, 2(3), 67–70.

Turner, M., & Engle, R. (1989). Is working memory capacity task dependent? *Journal of Memory and Language*, 28(2), 127–154.

Tweedy, J., & Lapinski, R. (1981). Facilitating word recognition: Evidence for strategic and automatic factors. *Quarterly Journal of Experimental Psychology: Human Experimental Psychology*, 33A(1), 51–59.

Vessey, I. (1987). On matching programmers' chunks with program structures: An empirical investigation. *International Journal of Man-Machine Studies*, 27(1), 65–89.

Vessey, I., & Weber, R. (1983). Some factors affecting program repair maintenance: An empirical study. *Communications of the ACM*, 26(2), 128–134.

Von Wright, J. (1970). On selection in visual immediate memory. *ACTA Psychologica*, 33, 280–292.

Waldrop, M. (1987). The working of working memory. Science, 237(4822), 1564–1567.

Weiser, M. (1982). Programmers use slices when debugging. *Communications of the ACM*, 25(7), 446–452.

Weizenbaum, J. (1976). *Computer Power and Human Reason*, W. H. Freeman and Company, San Francisco, Calif.

West, R., & Morris, C. (1985). Spatial cognition on nonspatial tasks: Finding spatial knowledge when you're not looking for it. In Cohen, R., Ed., *The Development of Spatial Cognition*, Lawrence Erlbaum Associates Publishers, Hillsdale, N. J.

Weyuker, E. (1988). Evaluating software complexity measures. *IEEE Transactions on Software Engineering*, 14(9), 1357–1365.

Weyuker, E., & Jeng, B. (1991). Analyzing partition testing strategies. *IEEE Transactions on Software Engineering*, 17(7), 703–711.

Wheeler, D. (1970). Processes in word recognition. *Cognitive Psychology*, 1, 59–85.

Winograd, T. (1983). *Language as a Cognitive Process*, Addison-Wesley Publishing Company, Reading, Mass.

Winograd, T., & Flores, F. (1986). *Understanding Computers and Cognition: A New Foundation for Design*, Addison-Wesley Publishing Company, Reading, Ma.

Winston, P. (1977). *Artificial Intelligence*, Addison-Wesley Publishing Company, Reading, Mass.

Woods, D., & Roth, E. (1988). Cognitive engineering: Human problem solving with tools. *Human Factors*, 30(4), 415–430.

Yantis, S., & Meyer, D. (1988). Dynamics of activation in semantic and episodic memory. *Journal of Experimental Psychology: General*, 117(2), 130–147.

Young, D., & Bellezza, F. (1982). Encoding variability, memory organization, and the repetition effect. *Journal of Experimental Psychology: Learning, Memory, and Cognition*, 9(6), 545–559.

Youngs, E. (1974). Human errors in programming. *International Journal of Man-Machine Studies*, 6, 361–376.

Zelkowitz, M. (1990). A functional correctness model of program verification. *Computer*, 23(11), 30–39.

Index